OCCASIO

G000155258

Back to the Future

Postwar Reconstruction and Stabilization in Lebanon

Edited by Sena Eken and Thomas Helbling

INTERNATIONAL MONETARY FUND
Washington DC
1999

© 1999 International Monetary Fund

Production: IMF Graphics Section
Figures: In-Ok Yoon
Typesetting: Julio R. Prego

Cataloging-in-Publication Data

Back to the future : postwar reconstruction and stabilization in Lebanon /
    edited by Sena Eken and Thomas Helbling. — Washington, D.C. : Interna-
tional Monetary Fund, 1999.
        p.   cm. — (Occasional paper, ISSN 0251-6365 ; no. 176)

    Includes bibliographical references.
    ISBN 1-55775-784-4

    1. Reconstruction — Lebanon.   2. Economic stabilization – Lebanon.
3. Finance, Public — Lebanon. 4. Fiscal policy — Lebanon.   5. Interest
rates — Lebanon.   6. Debts, Public — Lebanon.   7. European Union —
Lebanon.   8. Lebanon – Economic policy.   9. Lebanon – Economic conditions — Statistics.   I. Eken, Sena.   II. Helbling, Thomas.   III. International
Monetary Fund.   IV. Occasional paper (International Monetary Fund) ;
no. 176.
HC415.24.B22 1999

Price: US$18.00
(US$15.00 to full-time faculty members and
students at universities and colleges)

Please send orders to:
International Monetary Fund, Publication Services
700 19th Street, N.W., Washington, D.C. 20431, U.S.A.
Tel.: (202) 623-7430   Telefax: (202) 623-7201
E-mail: publications@imf.org
Internet: http://www.imf.org

recycled paper

Contents

Statistical Appendix Tables

The following symbols have been used throughout this paper:

. . .   to indicate that data are not available;

n.a.   to indicate not applicable;

—   to indicate that the figure is zero or less than half the final digit shown, or that the item does not exist;

–   between years or months (e.g., 1994–95 or January–June) to indicate the years or months covered, including the beginning and ending years or months;

/   between years (e.g., 1994/95) to indicate a crop or fiscal (financial) year.

"Billion" means a thousand million.

Minor discrepancies between constituent figures and totals are due to rounding.

The term "country," as used in this paper, does not in all cases refer to a territorial entity that is a state as understood by international law and practice; the term also covers some territorial entities that are not states, but for which statistical data are maintained and provided internationally on a separate and independent basis.

Preface

In this Occasional Paper, the progress of Lebanon's postwar reconstruction and stabilization efforts in the last five to six years are examined. The studies were prepared in conjunction with the 1997 Article IV consultation with Lebanon. They were updated in the fall of 1998 to take into account developments in the first half of the year, reflecting data and developments through June 1998.

The authors are grateful to the Lebanese authorities for their cooperation. His Excellency, Dr. Nasser Saidi, the Vice Governor of the Central Bank of Lebanon when the Occasional Paper was prepared and now Minister of Economy, Trade, and Industry, took a special interest in this project, and his comments and support are greatly appreciated. The authors would also like to thank Paul Chabrier and Mohamed El-Erian for their encouragement, Cyrus Sassanpour for valuable comments, Margaret Boesch, Deborah Chungu, Barbara Lissenburg, and Eleanor Wood for secretarial assistance, and Juanita Roushdy of the External Relations Department for editing the manuscript and coordinating publication.

The views expressed here, as well as any errors, are solely the responsibility of the authors and do not necessarily reflect the opinions of the Lebanese authorities, the IMF, or its Executive Directors.

1 Reconstruction and Stabilization— An Overview

Sena Eken

Following the end of Lebanon's civil war, which started in 1975 and spanned 15 years, the authorities began the difficult task of simultaneous economic stabilization and confidence building on the one hand, and postwar reconstruction and development on the other. To this end, the government took the lead in reconstruction by formulating first the National Emergency Reconstruction Program and subsequently the Horizon 2000 Program. Each aimed to rapidly rehabilitate and enhance the country's severely damaged infrastructure in preparation for private sector-led growth over the medium term. At the same time, to stabilize expectations and achieve rapid disinflation, an exchange-rate-based nominal anchor policy was adopted starting at the end of 1992.

The strategy, despite a difficult environment characterized by episodes of domestic political uncertainty, a fluid regional context, and limited external assistance for the reconstruction program, has been successful in several respects.

Growth. The end of the war allowed households, firms, and the government to return to normal conditions of production and consumption, which, in conjunction with the rebuilding of residential and business structures, the productive capacity of enterprises, the stock of consumer durables, and the government-led reconstruction program to build infrastructure, had the expected strongly positive effect on growth. During 1991–97, the average annual growth rate of GDP amounted to 9.7 percent, significantly improving per capita income (Figure 1.1). In 1996, the rate of economic growth slowed to 4 percent, adversely affected by the bombings in April and the decline in construction activities resulting from the excess supply in some segments of the real estate market; in 1997, the growth rate is estimated to have remained at that level as the contractionary impact of further declines in construction activity offset the increased service sector activity (e.g., tourism).

Inflation. Under the exchange-rate-based stabilization policy, the Lebanese pound (LL) appreciated from $0.544 per LL 1,000 at the end of 1992 to $0.660 per LL 1,000 at the end of June 1998 (Figure 1.2). The policy, supported by a prudent monetary policy, helped stabilize expectations and reduce inflation. The annual average inflation rate, which had increased from 52 percent in 1991 to 100 percent in 1992, declined rapidly once the nominal anchor policy was implemented and amounted to about 8 percent in 1997. With fiscal imbalances reduced and bottlenecks in the economy unclogged as reconstruction took hold, the average annual inflation rate slowed down further to about 5 percent during the first half of 1998.

Foreign exchange reserves. The exchange-rate-based nominal anchor policy was implemented by means of a supportive interest rate policy. High interest rates helped attract large capital inflows, which together with foreign investment into the real estate sector and financing for the reconstruction program, more than financed the external current account deficits and led to a sharp increase in foreign exchange reserves. Gross official reserves rose from $1.2 billion at the end of 1991 to over $6.1 billion (equivalent to about 10 months of imports) at the end of June 1998, while net foreign exchange reserves rose from $1.2 billion to over $3.2 billion (6.9 months of imports) during the same period.

Dollarization. The decline in inflation, the stable exchange rate, and the buildup of reserves accompanied by the authorities' increased credibility in financial markets raised the demand for Lebanese pounds. As a result, dollarization, measured by the share of foreign currency deposits in total liquidity, declined from a maximum of 68 percent in mid-1993 to 53 percent by the end of 1996. Although dollarization increased slightly in the second half of 1997, as pressures on reserves emerged with the crises in Asia and uncertainty increased with regard to domestic public finances, the favorable trend was reestablished in May–June 1998 and the dollarization started to decline again.

Structural improvements. Favorable macroeconomic and financial developments were accompanied by structural improvements. A significant part of the infrastructure has been restored; the private sector has been getting more involved in reconstruction including through build-operate-transfer schemes; the financial sector has been deepened and

Figure 1.1. Selected Economic Indicators

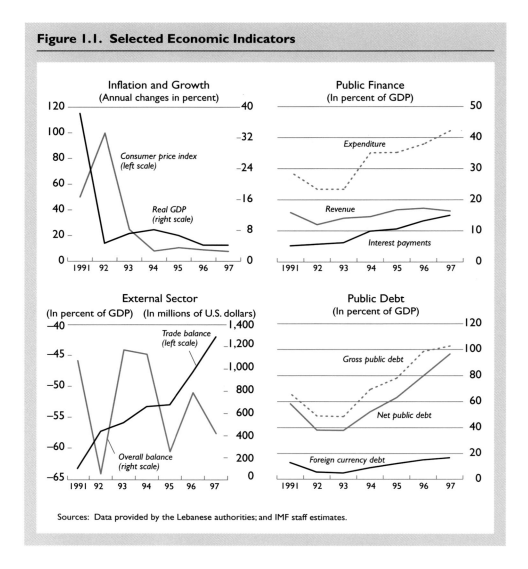

Sources: Data provided by the Lebanese authorities; and IMF staff estimates.

widened, its supervision and capital base have been strengthened; and the budget process and administration have been streamlined and modernized, and revenue administration has been strengthened. Furthermore, the government and the private sector were able to tap international capital markets. Structural improvement in the economy increased productivity and helped compensate for the effects of the real effective exchange rate appreciation on competitiveness, which is more limited in Lebanon than in other countries given the highly dollarized nature of the economy.

Nevertheless, the conflicting claims of reconstruction and stabilization requirements have proven to be more challenging than envisaged.

Public finance and debt. Rebuilding the infrastructure and providing regular public services have been the government's crucial contribution to the recon-

struction effort. However, the acceleration in the growth of government capital expenditure, together with large and expanding current expenditure and the slow recovery of the revenue-generation capacity, has led to sizable fiscal imbalances. While the deficit fell from 16 percent of GDP in 1991 to 8 percent in 1993, it rose and remained high thereafter; in 1997, it amounted to about 26 percent. The deficits have been financed mostly through the issuance of government papers (with maturities of up to two years) denominated in Lebanese pounds and held primarily by the domestic banking system. Consequently, the public debt increased rapidly. During 1993–97, gross public debt, as a percent of GDP, increased from 49 percent to 103 percent, and net public debt rose from 38 percent to 97 percent. Determined efforts to turn around the fiscal situation and stabilize the debt dynamics were made in 1998. To these ends, the 1998

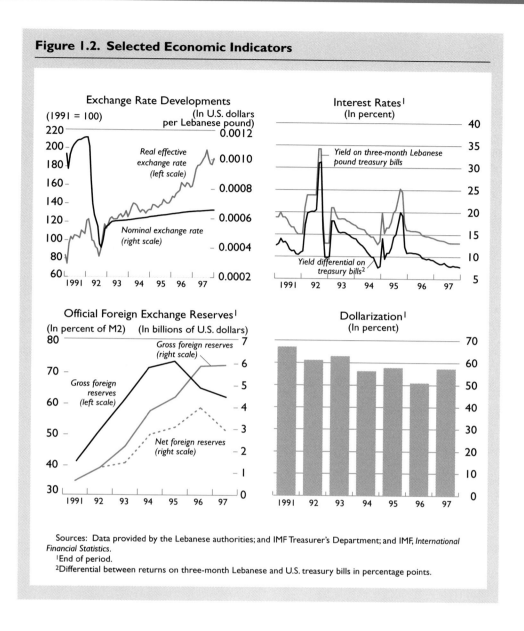

Figure 1.2. Selected Economic Indicators

Sources: Data provided by the Lebanese authorities; and IMF Treasurer's Department; and IMF, *International Financial Statistics*.

[1]End of period.

[2]Differential between returns on three-month Lebanese and U.S. treasury bills in percentage points.

budget involved both expenditure and revenue measures to initiate the front-loaded adjustment needed to ensure medium-term sustainability and underpin a soft landing. Furthermore, the mobilization of external financing has eased interest costs on the budget and allowed for lengthening the maturity structure of public debt. The budgetary outcome during the first half of 1998 confirms the government's determined efforts to achieve fiscal adjustment and bring down the overall deficit to the budgeted level of 15 percent of GDP; during January–June 1998, the cumulative deficit as a percent of expenditures was well within the 1998 budget target and significantly below the outcomes observed in 1996 and 1997. The continua-

tion of these developments will ease strains on the overall macroeconomic policy mix and reduce the vulnerability of the budget to changes in financial market sentiments.

Interest rates. The large financing needs of the government with the nominal exchange rate anchor policy involved high and flexible interest rates. Over time, the authorities gained credibility in financial markets, which was reflected in the gradual decline in nominal and real interest rates and in the differential with respect to comparable U.S. dollar-denominated assets in 1996–97. Notwithstanding recent declines in nominal interest rates, the cost of servicing the growing stock of debt has been high and increasing: interest payments absorbed 90 percent of total budgetary revenues in 1997. Moreover, high interest rates have adversely affected private sector activity.

External imbalances. The return to less trying conditions after the war took place in the context of marked divergence between current and anticipated future income streams, accompanied by domestic demand in excess of current capacity. The natural result of this divergence has been borrowing against future income as well as dissaving. Borrowing occurred not only by the government as discussed above, but also by firms. Meanwhile, dissavings and transfers (external assets) have been prevalent at the households level. Reflecting these saving-investment imbalances, large trade and external current account deficits accompanied reconstruction and the postwar normalization of economic activity. While the size of the current account deficit is subject to severe measurement problems, the occurrence of large financial inflows in the form of transfers, foreign direct investment, and portfolio flows, including from the large community of Lebanese expatriates, cannot be doubted. These large inflows, induced in part by high interest rates and exchange rate stability, made the economy more vulnerable to shifts in market sentiments. The vulnerability was well managed. The large amounts of foreign exchange reserves, which covered a significant share of public short-term domestic currency liabilities, supported the authorities' efforts to keep market sentiments in check. Moreover, data on identifiable gross external assets and liabilities of resident units (public sector including central bank, commercial banks, and nonbank private sector) indicate that assets exceeded liabilities by about a factor 2 at the end of 1997;[1] this suggests that the Lebanese economy is still in a net creditor position vis-à-vis the rest of the world despite the large cumulative current account deficit of the last few years. The net creditor position certainly contributed to the remarkable success of foreign currency bond issues by both government and private entities in international capital markets.

Challenges ahead. The main challenge for the years to come is to ensure the sustainability of the success in the reconstruction and the stabilization of the economy and to enhance the framework for a path of rapid and balanced growth. In this context, fiscal consolidation remains the most urgent policy issue in view of the debt dynamics and the need to crowd in private sector activity. This would involve not only a front-loaded reduction in the deficit and surpluses in the primary balance in the coming years, but also improvements in the structure of the budget, especially through reducing the dependency on customs revenues. The latter is particularly important in light of the envisaged Association Agreement with the European Union and the intention to reestablish Lebanon as a regional hub for trade in goods and services in the Middle East. The front-loaded fiscal adjustment and the improvements in the structure of the budget would be facilitated by the early introduction of a general sales tax, cost-recovery measures related to public infrastructure services, and continued efforts in strengthening tax administration. In addition to a stable macroeconomic environment and low production costs, institutions and regulatory reforms are needed to create an enabling environment for private-sector-led high growth over the medium term. High private-sector-led growth should increase employment opportunities and alleviate poverty. Nevertheless, there is also a need to address disparities in income distribution and regional socioeconomic differentials to enhance the sociopolitical acceptability of the medium-term adjustment and reform process.

The challenges facing the Lebanese economy in an environment of globalized financial markets are well recognized by the authorities. Determined implementation of fiscal adjustment and reforms holds the promise of virtuous cycles of economic stability and high growth in Lebanon, providing for increased opportunities for employment and higher standards of living.

Against this background, the sections that follow aim to contribute to the analysis of recent developments in the Lebanese economy and its policy challenges in the medium term. The analysis is based on information and data up to June 1998.

Section II reviews the evolution of Lebanon's public investment program over the reconstruction period, including its size, phasing, composition, and financing. In addition, it discusses cost recovery and the role of the private sector in the reconstruction, both of which have implications for policies aimed at fostering the economy's full long-term growth potential.

Section III discusses the evolutions and the structure of Lebanon's public finances, a key determinant of the country's financial outlook. In this context, it analyzes the issue of fiscal sustainability in Lebanon, focusing on (1) the adjustment in the primary deficit that is needed for the debt dynamics to become consistent with solvency and medium-term macroeconomic stability, and (2) the adjustment in the structure of the expenditure and revenue that should be targeted to maximize their positive growth effects and reduce their vulnerability to exogenous shocks and structural changes in the economy.

Section IV reviews the evolution of Lebanese pound interest rates, key variables for both monetary

---

[1]Short-term gross external assets exceeded short-term external liabilities by a factor of 4.5.

policy and public finances, and analyzes their determinants. The analysis focuses on factors that explain the interest rate differential between comparable assets denominated in Lebanese pounds and in U.S. dollars, which have remained large and positive despite the gradual and steady appreciation of the Lebanese pound against the U.S. currency.

Section V presents an overview of Lebanon's public debt structure and analyzes the policy problems associated with it, in particular the interaction between public debt management and monetary policy. It then discusses theoretical aspects of public debt management and applies it to the Lebanese case.

Section VI describes the institutional structure of the Lebanese financial system and discusses the impact of recent reforms on financial deepening, the soundness of the banking system and the development of financial markets. Given the progress to date, it considers the elements needed to enhance the role of the financial system in mobilizing domestic and foreign savings and ensuring their efficient allocation, as well as to achieve the authorities' objective of reestablishing Beirut as a regional financial center.

Section VII discusses Lebanon's current relationship with the European Union and potential modifications under the envisaged Association Agreement. After reviewing the implications of an Association Agreement with the EU, it focuses on the liberalization of trade in services—an area from which Lebanon can reap significant benefits.

II Public Investment Planning and Progress

John Wetter

The civil war had a devastating effect on the social fabric and the domestic economy of Lebanon. By the end of the war, it is estimated that the country had lost nearly half of its physical capital stock. Coupled with an equally serious loss of human capital, per capita income had fallen to about one-third of the prewar peak. The rehabilitation of the public infrastructure therefore became key in the government's efforts to support the postwar recovery.

To this end, the government revived the Council for Development and Reconstruction (CDR) at the end of 1990 and entrusted it with the task of preparing a national reconstruction strategy and implementing a National Emergency Recovery Program (NERP). NERP, a short-term program (1993–97) originally costed at $2.25 billion (1992 prices), was designed to rehabilitate key physical and social infrastructure. Subsequently, CDR developed a broader, longer term (1993–2002) investment program by building on NERP. This new *Horizon 2000* program augmented the annual investment expenditures of NERP. It aimed at better sectoral and regional balance, and the expansion of key sectoral infrastructures, in addition to a general rehabilitation of infrastructure.

The Horizon 2000 Program

Horizon 2000 went beyond the initial emergency works of NERP and included the rehabilitation and expansion of infrastructure and public facilities so as to lay the foundations for future economic growth. In its 1995 version, Horizon 2000 envisaged total public investments of $17.7 billion between 1995 and 2007 valued at 1995 prices (estimated at $22.2 billion in current prices). By sector, planned investments were:
- physical infrastructure (electricity, telecommunications, roads, highways), 37 percent;
- social infrastructure (primary, secondary, vocational and technical education; culture; health; social affairs; housing and resettlement), 25 percent;
- public services (water, waste, public transport, railways), 22 percent;
- productive sectors (agriculture and irrigation, industry and oil, airport, ports, free zones, tourism, private sector services), 8 percent; and
- state apparatus (government buildings, security forces, public information, rehabilitation of public administration), 8 percent.

The envisaged investment program was considerably front-loaded. During the three-year period 1995–97, over $6 billion in capital outlays were intended—more than one-third of total public investment expenditures envisaged for the entire, extended Horizon 2000 period through 2007. Subsequent revisions, taking into consideration slippages in actual implementation and rephasing, reduced intended capital outlays during the same period to approximately $4.6 billion. Realized contracts were even less. For the period January 1, 1992 through December 31, 1997, $4.2 billion in contracts were awarded, of which $932 million have been completed: an additional $1.4 billion in project contracts were in preparation as of January 1998 (Table 2.1[1]).

The macroeconomic model underlying the Horizon 2000 program implied private sector investments of nearly $42 billion between 1995 and 2007, more than twice the size of the public program. The basis of the assumption was historical data suggesting that the private sector had traditionally accounted for around 85 percent of Lebanon's GDP. GDP growth over the 13-year period was expected to be on the order of 8 percent a year, sufficient to double per capita GDP by the end of the program. The public finance scenario of Horizon 2000 was based on a fiscal adjustment process that was expected to yield a zero primary current balance in 1999 and a surplus thereafter, which would rise to more than 8 percent of GDP by 2007. Indeed, these cumulative budget surpluses after 2000 were seen as becoming the principal source of financing for both

---

[1]Because of data constraints, it is not possible to present identical time periods across tables.

Table 2.1. Horizon 2000 Program: Sectoral Distribution of Actual and Projected Public Expenditures, Contracts Awarded, and Contracts in Preparation

(In millions of U.S. dollars)

	Horizon 2000		Contracts Awarded, Jan. 1, 1992–Dec. 31, 1997			Additional Contracts in Preparation
	1993–94	1995–97	Completed	In progress	Total	
Physical infrastructure	626.5	3,173.2	601.9	2,204.2	2,806.0	345.6
Electricity	255.2	1,205.3	372.3	908.8	1,281.0	74.5
Telecommunications	201.9	495.2	138.0	484.4	622.4	52.8
Roads¹	113.4	930.6	81.3	294.9	376.2	216.5
Airport and ports	56.1	542.2	10.3	516.1	526.4	1.8
Social infrastructure	217.6	1,710.0	104.4	447.8	553.2	163.7
Education	80.0	871.7	96.7	326.3	422.9	69.5
Public health and social affairs	3.5	275.2	4.9	115.3	121.3	92.7
Housing and resettlement	134.0	532.7	2.5	1.7	4.2	0.0
Environment	0.2	30.4	0.3	4.5	4.8	1.5
Public services	113.6	864.6	102.7	512.7	615.4	692.8
Water supply and wastewater	96.7	665.8	55.9	341.7	397.6	593.2
Solid waste	15.1	124.6	46.8	171.0	217.8	99.6
Productive sectors	51.2	316.1	14.9	27.4	42.2	45.1
Agriculture and irrigation	50.1	163.3	14.1	25.1	39.1	34.1
Industry, oil, and gas	1.0	152.7	0.8	2.3	3.1	11.0
State apparatus	46.2	220.6	108.4	101.7	210.3	176.6
Government buildings	41.1	171.9	18.8	62.9	81.8	82.5
Management and implementation	5.2	48.7	89.6	38.8	128.5	94.1
Total	1,055.1	6,284.5	932.3	3,293.8	4,227.1	1,423.8

Source: CDR, "Progress Report, Update January 1998" (Beirut: Council for Development and Reconstruction).
¹Including public transport.

public investment and debt service (Table 2.2). The overall budget was envisaged to be balanced by 2004 and to generate a surplus large enough to achieve financial self-sufficiency by 2006. Total debt (domestic and foreign) was projected to average just under 70 percent of GDP over the period, peaking at 91 percent in 1999. According to the scenario, total debt-service payments as a percentage of GDP would consistently remain below 10 percent during the whole period, with a downward trend starting in 2002.

As actual macroeconomic and financing developments during the past three years turned out to be different from what was envisaged, some changes in the program have occurred. Such a reassessment of priorities was to be expected; indeed, the government has always stressed that while it intends to broadly follow the original program, Horizon 2000 is not a rigid, unchanging blueprint, but rather a framework for reconstruction and development.

Phase I Achievements and Phase II Priorities

Three years into the revised Horizon 2000, the first phase of rehabilitation is nearing completion, and a number of major benefits are already being experienced: 24-hour electricity supplies are provided to most users; telecommunication systems are functioning better; some 1,200 public schools have been rehabilitated; and many water supply systems throughout the country have received emergency repairs. Garbage collection in Beirut has been in place for over three years and is being extended to other regions. Significant progress has been made in renewing roads and services in the northern and southern suburbs of Beirut. Continued extensive work to water and telecommunication systems is also under way; work has begun on a number of major new development projects, including new power-generating facilities, Beirut University Hospital, Beirut International Airport, expansion of the Lebanese University, and urgently required roads projects.

Table 2.2. Horizon 2000 Program: Original Financing Scenario

	1995–2000		2001–2007		Total	
	In millions of U.S. dollars	In percent	In millions of U.S. dollars	In percent	In millions of U.S. dollars	In percent
Foreign grants	0.3	2.2	0.0	0.0	0.3	1.0
Foreign loans	8.2	61.2	3.0	17.0	11.2	36.1
Domestic borrowing	4.7	35.1	2.5	14.2	7.2	23.2
Budget surpluses	0.2	1.5	12.1	68.8	12.3	39.7
Total	13.4	100.0	17.6	100.0	31.0	100.0

Sources: CDR; and World Bank.

Having concentrated on basic infrastructure during Phase I, CDR is now, in Phase II, turning attention to social infrastructure (in particular, education and health), water supply, wastewater, and solid waste sectors. Estimates of Phase II programs vary, but investments on the order of $5 billion over five years are foreseen.

In December 1996, the government presented a set of "high-priority projects" to the "Friends of Lebanon" conference, a forum of donor countries. With a total cost of about $5 billion, the 31 projects and programs focused on roads ($1.25 billion), water ($1.2 billion), environment ($850 million), education ($800 million), agriculture ($400 million), health ($100 million), and other ($400 million).

Financing Strategy

The financing strategy for the reconstruction program aims at maximizing the use of external finance, preferably on concessional terms, to contain the government's domestic debt and avoid absorbing excessive amounts of local resources to the detriment of the private sector. External finance for the reconstruction program obtained thus far includes grants and soft loans, commercial loans with export guarantees, and private financing as part of projects to be operated by private firms.[2] According to CDR, as of December 31, 1997, "documented" foreign funding for Lebanon's reconstruction program from the beginning of NERP amounted to the equivalent of $4.0 billion, with $0.5 billion in grants and $3.5 billion in loans[3] (Table 2.3). Much of this financing relates to

projects that have not yet started and for which contracts have yet to be signed. Of the $4.2 billion in current or completed contracts indicated in Table 2.1, $2.0 billion (47 percent) is foreign-funded. Twenty-four bilateral and multilateral donors, and a number of commercial banks are providing funding. Four financing sources account for more than half the total.

Although the government had hoped to receive commitments for the full $5 billion priority program from donors at the Friends of Lebanon conference, donors pledged only $3.2 billion. Of this amount, $1 billion was short-term funding; the remaining $2.2 billion was in longer-term commitments. Additional unspecified commitments were made in the form of concessional export credit facilities and loan guarantees.

In addition to its responsibility for mobilizing grants and loans from official creditors, CDR seeks financing through commercial credits guaranteed by export credit agencies. So far, at least three major electricity sector projects have been financed by such commercial credits: Zahrani and Beddawi combined cycle-power stations, gas turbine electricity generators at Sour and Baalbek, and the extension of the electricity transmission network.

Private operating concessions (except for the contracts with the cellular telephone networks negotiated in August 1994 by the Ministry of Posts and Telecommunications in collaboration with CDR, see below) are the responsibility of the Investment Development Authority of Lebanon (IDAL). Established in 1994 for, among other things, assisting foreign investors and promoting build-operate-transfer and similar private financing schemes, IDAL has been given the responsibility for negotiating contracts for some facilities at the airport, the commercial center in Sports City, the free zones, the Arab Highway, and the northern and southern sections of the Beirut ring road. A listing of projects currently

---

[2]In addition, as discussed in Section V, Lebanon has turned to international capital markets for general budget financing through the issuance of Eurobonds (and other foreign currency bonds).

[3]The foreign financing presented in Table 2.3 excludes the foreign currency bonds, as well as the financing provided by the two cellular telephone network operators (estimated at around $150 million).

Table 2.3. Horizon 2000 Program: "Documented" Foreign Funding as of December 31, 1997

	In Millions of U.S. Dollars	In Percent
World Bank	598.3	14.9
Arab Fund for Economic and Social Development	503.6	12.6
European Investment Bank	499.8	12.5
Italy	340.1	8.5
France	272.9	6.8
Saudi Fund for Development	230.0	5.7
Kuwait Fund for Arab Economic Development	229.1	5.7
Islamic Development Bank	176.6	4.4
Commission of the European Union	170.3	4.3
Saudi Arabia	160.1	4.0
Japan	111.2	2.8
Spain	105.0	2.6
Germany	77.3	1.9
Kuwait	44.3	1.1
United Nations Secretariat and Agencies	43.0	1.1
Mediterranean Environmental Technical Assistance Program	34.2	0.9
International Fund for Agricultural Development	30.8	0.8
Abu Dhabi Fund for Development	25.0	0.6
OPEC Fund for International Development	24.2	0.6
Oman	15.0	0.4
China	6.0	0.1
United Arab Emirates	5.0	0.1
Conseil Regional d'Ile de France	1.7	0.0
Belgium	1.4	0.0
Qatar	1.0	0.0
Various Commercial Banks	297.8	7.4
Total	4,003.7	100.0

Source: CDR, "Progress Report, Update January 1998" (Beirut: Council for Development and Reconstruction, 1998).

available for private participation is shown in Table 2.4.

Private Sector Provision of Infrastructure

With major donor support beyond the levels indicated at the Friends of Lebanon conference unlikely, Lebanon will have to consider other options for financing necessary reconstruction works. The most likely solution will lie in increased private sector involvement through build-operate-transfer and similar schemes and privatization, and, for infrastructure and services remaining within the domain of the public sector, greater cost recovery.

Build-operate-transfer, build-operate-own, and similar schemes have already been used to finance two cellular telephone networks totaling 500,000 lines, parts of the airport, a major road project, and several smaller projects in the tourism sector. Solid waste collection in Beirut is handled by a private contractor, and, under the aegis of IDAL, a number of other build-operate-transfer projects have been proposed and are under discussion with potential investors (Table 2.4). At some point, however, the government may need to consider even greater private sector involvement.

The efficiency of resource allocation in the provision of private goods will be heightened if the private sector is the prime mover of investment and management, while government's role is concentrated on policy development and establishment, and enforcement of the regulatory environment. Efficiency stems from the discipline imposed by commercial principles and competition. The efficiency principal strongly suggests that the private sector should be providing infrastructure services in power, telecommunications, ports, railroads, parts of roads, water and wastewater, and solid-waste management. Serious considerations are warranted in this regard, particularly in view of the still limited, albeit

Table 2.4. Government Projects Available to Private Investors
(In millions of U.S. dollars)

Project	Investment Cost	Type of Contract[1]
IDAL, contracts awarded		
Airport car park	20	BOT
Airport catering and restaurants	31	BOT
Airport duty-free shops	180	OT
Airport fuel facilities	48	OT
Beirut sports city commercial center	150	BOT
Subtotal	429	
IDAL, bids under evaluation/negotiation		
Airport hotel	30	DBOT
Airport cargo handling buildings	15	BOT
Subtotal	45	
IDAL, in preparation		
Airport free zone	42	DBOT
Al-Quleaat "Rene Mouawad" Airport and free zone (Tripoli)	72	DBOT
Riyak Airport and free zone (Bekaa)	65	DBOT
Beirut International Culture and Conference Center	350	
Lebanon toll highway network	945	BOT
Subtotal	1,474	
Sidon Free Port, in preparation		
Infrastructure	300	DBF
Superstructure	230	OT
Subtotal	530	
Development of the northern coastline (LINORD)		
Bids under evaluation	550	
CDR, bids under evaluation/negotiation		
Underground car park, Grand Serail	6	BOT
Underground car park, Martyrs Square	30	BOT
Subtotal	36	
CDR, bids in preparation		
Cultural, commercial, parking complex, Tripoli	12	BOT
Ras Beirut Commercial Center	28	BOT
Subtotal	40	
Total	3,104	
Contracts awarded	429	
Bids under evaluation/negotiation	631	
In preparation	2,044	

Sources: IDAL, "Government Projects Available to Private Investors" (Beirut; Investment Development Authority of Lebanon, August 20, 1997); and updated information from IDAL Internet site.

[1]BOT: build-operate-transfer; OT: operate-transfer; DBOT: design-build-operate-transfer; and DBF: design-build-finance.

strengthened, institutional capacity and financial resources of the government in the postwar period.

Transition to private ownership of infrastructure will require careful sequencing. It requires establishing a proper regulatory framework to ensure competition, preventing natural monopolies, and protecting investor and consumer interests, as well as unbundling vertically integrated monopolies, and commercializing and corporatizing sectors before privatization can begin. So far, Lebanon does not have such a regulatory framework; indeed, some observers believe that a change in the constitution would be required before privatization could proceed.

It appears that the government has, thus far, opted for the approach of phased privatization in the major sectors, beginning with management and provision of infrastructure services and proceeding to ownership in the medium to long term. This phased privatization approach, while affording the government time to establish an appropriate legal and regulatory framework and effect restructuring requirements in the major infrastructure sectors, increases the burden of large recurrent expenditures with inevitable trade-offs for social and other expenditures.

In the power sector, the government has agreed on a program of sector-wide restructuring and reform actions designed to introduce competition and private sector participation in utility operations, as well as to reorganize Electricité du Liban (EDL).[4] Elements of the program include unbundling the vertically integrated EDL into separate production, transmission, and distribution functions; establishing several privately operated regional distribution concessions; introducing new laws providing for the separation of electricity generation, transmission, and distribution functions and the establishment of an autonomous regulatory agency; adopting a vigorous program to drastically cut nontechnical losses (currently over 40 percent of production is lost) and to improve collections; implementing revenue-sharing arrangements with private sector companies pursuant to which the private operators would lease or operate certain assets of EDL; and gradually phasing out government subsidies.

In addition to EDL, the government currently owns several major companies, including Société des Eaux de Beyrouth, the airport, and port companies, all of which offer—to varying degrees—opportunities for restructuring and greater private sector involvement.[5] Considerations have been given to, and contracts signed for, immediate and outright privatization for the capacity expansion under build-operate-transfer and build-operate-own arrangements and the provision of ancillary services in some sectors.

An important proportion of the infrastructure projects in the investment program provides "private" goods (electricity, telecommunications, and parts of transport, for example) in which users can be identified. An appropriate structure of user prices is of the foremost importance both from the viewpoint of resource allocation and financing. If there is full-cost recovery, an investment project would be budget neutral, and would strengthen the sustainability of the program.

Cost recovery for public investment can be achieved in two ways: first, indirect cost recovery through economic growth and the resultant tax base expansion; and second, direct cost recovery through charging prices for the sale of goods or services. While estimates vary, overall cost recovery could yield revenues in the range of 2 to 5 percent of the accumulated level of investment of GDP in the medium term, depending on the degree of success in restructuring the infrastructure sectors and in establishing cost-recovery mechanisms.

Conclusions

Implementation of Lebanon's public investment program began within the context of pressing needs for postwar infrastructure reconstruction and social services, on the one hand, and a fragile macroeconomy on the other. It was important for the government to move quickly to implement the reconstruction program and deliver social services. Now, the first phase of rehabilitation is nearing completion; basic infrastructure has been reconstructed throughout the country, and attention is being placed on "social infrastructure," in particular, education, health; water supply, wastewater, and solid waste. Approximately $5 billion in investments are foreseen over the coming five years.

Nevertheless, in view of the overall macroeconomic situation and the limited, albeit improving, implementation and funding capacities of the government, issues that have faced the authorities from the beginning of the reconstruction program still require attention. These include prioritization and phasing of the public investment program, the recurrent expenditure requirements, and cost-recovery mechanisms.

Furthermore, in each sector underlying questions remain as to the proper public/private sector balance in the provision of infrastructure and other goods and services. Additional issues pertain to the sequencing of sectoral and administrative reforms and to the establishment of appropriate legal and regulatory frameworks, particularly as greater private sector participation is sought. Recent and prospective developments in the restructuring of EDL offers a potential model for other sectors.

The macroeconomic consistency of the public investment program also depends on the degree to which the program demands future budgetary resources, both through incremental operation-and-maintenance expenditures and through debt service (to the extent that projects are financed with debt). These recurrent expenditure requirements could prove to be very substantial in the Lebanese context owing to the sheer size of the reconstruction program and if the newly installed capacity is to be adequately maintained. The associated demands on budgetary resources could be minimized by greater private sector participation in the provision of infrastructure services and by establishing appropriate cost-recovery mechanisms wherever the beneficiaries can be clearly identified.

---

[4]A Power Sector Restructuring and Transmission Expansion Project has been agreed on between the government and the World Bank.

[5]Banque du Liban also owns significant commercial assets, including the shares of the national air carrier, Middle East Airlines.

III   Postwar Reconstruction, Public Finances, and Fiscal Sustainability

Thomas Helbling

Since the end of the civil war, Lebanon has embarked on an ambitious program of economic reconstruction and stabilization. A rapid rehabilitation and enhancement of the country's infrastructure was an essential component of the government's policy strategy. Accordingly, the government's program envisaged sharp increases in capital expenditure and large primary budget deficits, which would be largely financed through capital markets. The primary deficits were expected to reverse rapidly to a primary surplus as (1) the infrastructure rehabilitation would ignite private-sector-led growth with a correspondingly expanding tax base, (2) the strengthening of the administrative infrastructure would foster fast recovery of the tax administration and its revenue-collection capacity, and (3) the increases in capital expenditure would be transitory and reversed upon completion of the infrastructure rehabilitation. Therefore, it was anticipated that the upper limit of the debt-to-GDP ratio would be reached soon during the reconstruction.

A policy strategy that involves borrowing in anticipation of higher, future permanent income is reasonable during a reconstruction period, particularly for the government, which should suffer less from financial market imperfections than private households and firms. As pointed out by Barro (1979) and others, borrowing allows for tax smoothing, that is, the temporary debt financing of spending during a period of revenue below its long-term average. In the context of Lebanon's reconstruction, debt financing has allowed for significant capital expenditure and for the gradual rehabilitation of the revenue system and administration.

During 1991–97, the government succeeded in rehabilitating a significant part of the country's infrastructure, and the reconstruction program has been one of the forces underlying the rapid economic growth during the period. Managing the fiscal implications of the reconstruction, however, has been a major challenge in the context of the stabilization policy and given problems associated with larger-than-expected current expenditure and a slower-than-anticipated recovery of the revenue administration and collection capacity. Under these circumstances, the anticipated rapid reversal in the primary budget balance did not materialize and budget deficits remained large—varying between 9 percent of GDP in 1993 and about 26 percent in 1997. Consequently, net public debt increased from a low of 38 percent of GDP at the end of 1993 to about 97 percent at the end of 1997.

In light of these large deficits and the associated rapid increase in public debt, questions about the implications of the current fiscal policy stance on the debt dynamics and macroeconomic stability in Lebanon have arisen. The delay in the adjustment of the primary balance has increased the adjustment needed to stabilize the debt dynamics as depicted in the stylized scenario in Figure 3.1. The delay not only shifts the debt path upward but also changes its slope as a result of the increasing interest burden incurred by the growing debt. A fiscal adjustment path that would have been sufficient to ensure stabilization of the debt dynamics earlier can become inadequate later.

The government has recognized the challenges posed by the delayed adjustment in the primary government balance and the growth in the public debt. With the 1997 budget, which envisaged a reduction in the primary budget balance by about 7 percentage points from the 7.6 percent of GDP registered in 1996, another attempt was made toward fiscal adjustment. The actual outcome, however, was once more disappointing as the budget deficit in percent of GDP increased instead of decreasing and the rapid accumulation of public debt continued. The medium-term adjustment to ensure fiscal sustainability thus became a major policy issue in late 1997 when the 1998 budget was being prepared.

In 1998, the government made a determined attempt to turn around the fiscal situation and stabilize the public debt dynamics. Learning from past problems, the government included in the budget, for the first time since 1995, not only expenditure but also revenue measures so as to initiate the adjustment needed to ensure medium-term fiscal sustainability. Based on information about the actual budgetary outcome during the first half of the year, chances for achieving the budgetary targets of 1998 are good.

Figure 3.1. Fiscal Shocks and Delayed Adjustment
(In percent of GDP)

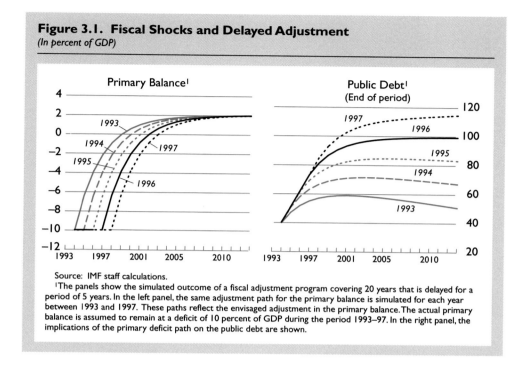

Source: IMF staff calculations.

[1]The panels show the simulated outcome of a fiscal adjustment program covering 20 years that is delayed for a period of 5 years. In the left panel, the same adjustment path for the primary balance is simulated for each year between 1993 and 1997. These paths reflect the envisaged adjustment in the primary balance. The actual primary balance is assumed to remain at a deficit of 10 percent of GDP during the period 1993–97. In the right panel, the implications of the primary deficit path on the public debt are shown.

Doing so would prepare the ground for successful fiscal adjustment in the medium term.

Lebanon's Public Finances— An Overview

For many years, large budget deficits and a rapidly growing public debt have been the most important macroeconomic problems faced by the authorities. For a full appreciation of the current policy issues, the origins and evolution of the current fiscal problems need to be ascertained. As shown below, these problems can be traced to the fiscal disarray that resulted from the war years and the delays in implementing the planned fiscal adjustment after 1993.

Fiscal Policies and Budgetary Performance, 1972–97

Before the war, the government had a limited role in the economy.[1] The country was well known for its conservative fiscal policies with low expenditure and low tax ratios, in a macroeconomic environment characterized by a stable currency, low inflation,

sustained economic growth, and overall balance of payments surpluses. The civil war has had a profound impact on the level and structure of public finances in Lebanon, and, consequently, large fiscal deficits have become a chronic problem. Since the end of the war, the reconstruction needs coupled with a weak initial administrative capacity have only compounded the fiscal challenges that Lebanon has been facing.

The War Legacy

The war had four main effects on public finances. First, the general breakdown in government authority had a dramatic effect on the revenue-collection capability, and revenue plummeted from levels of more than 15 percent of GDP to levels that were generally below 10 percent (Table 3.1). The effects of the loss of control over the ports were particularly important because customs revenue was the main source of tax revenue.[2] Second, the stagnant and irregular economic activity reinforced the decrease in collected revenue. Third, the accelerating inflation led to an erosion of real revenue as a result of the tax collection lags (often referred to as the Tanzi effect). Fourth, government expenditure, as a percentage of GDP, rose above 20 percent on account of the au-

[1]See Saidi (1989) and Eken and others (1995, Section III) on fiscal developments in Lebanon since 1974.

[2]See Makdisi (1987) for a detailed discussion.

Table 3.1. Government Operations[1]

	Selected Prewar Years			Selected War Years								Postwar Years				
	1972	1974	1975	1976	1980	1985	1988	1989	1990	1991	1992	1993	1994	1995	1996	1997
							(In percent of GDP)									
Revenue	12.1	15.6	10.7	3.7	13.7	7.3	1.8	6.8	9.7	15.9	12.0	14.1	14.6	16.8	17.3	16.4
Tax revenue	8.0	11.5	7.5	2.0	9.5	2.0	0.6	1.4	2.1	5.4	5.4	9.3	9.4	11.1	14.0	12.6
Indirect taxes	5.6	8.9	6.4	1.9	7.0	0.9	0.1	0.3	0.2	3.2	4.9	7.5	7.6	9.5	12.4	10.7
Of which: customs duties	2.4	2.6	1.1	0.2	2.4	1.1	0.5	1.1	0.1	2.4	3.4	5.0	5.2	7.3	8.0	7.5
Direct taxes	2.4	2.6	1.1	0.2	2.4	1.1	0.5	1.1	1.9	2.2	0.5	1.8	1.8	1.6	1.6	2.0
Nontax revenue	4.1	4.1	3.1	1.7	4.3	5.3	1.2	5.5	7.6	10.5	6.6	4.8	5.2	5.7	3.3	3.8
Expenditure	15.4	15.0	13.6	15.7	27.1	43.1	19.2	39.1	39.4	28.9	23.4	23.4	35.1	35.2	37.9	42.2
Current expenditures	12.1	12.4	7.6	12.6	20.9	39.5	17.8	36.7	37.8	25.1	21.8	20.0	25.8	25.7	29.4	33.6
Wages and salaries	...	...	...	...	8.5	7.4	4.5	7.2	10.6	9.0	6.9	9.9	11.2	10.4	11.1	10.8
Other current	...	...	...	...	10.8	12.4	4.5	10.9	14.0	10.3	7.9	4.2	3.3	3.8	4.4	7.4
Interest payments	...	...	...	...	1.5	9.9	5.9	11.3	10.8	5.0	5.5	6.0	9.7	10.4	13.0	14.8
Domestic	...	...	...	...	1.5	9.8	5.8	11.2	10.3	4.9	4.8	5.7	9.6	9.7	12.1	14.1
Foreign	...	...	...	...	0.1	0.1	0.1	0.1	0.5	0.0	0.7	0.2	0.1	0.7	0.9	0.7
Electricité du Liban fuel subsidy	...	...	...	...	...	9.8	2.9	7.4	2.3	0.8	1.5	0.0	1.6	1.2	1.0	0.7
Capital expenditures	3.3	2.6	6.1	3.1	6.3	3.6	1.4	2.4	1.7	3.9	1.5	3.4	9.3	9.4	8.5	8.6
Overall balance (excluding grants)	-3.3	0.6	-3.0	-12.0	-13.4	-35.8	-17.4	-32.3	-29.8	-13.1	-11.4	-9.2	-20.5	-18.4	-20.6	-25.8
Financing	3.3	-0.6	3.0	12.0	13.4	35.8	17.4	33.3	26.6	15.7	10.3	9.8	20.5	18.6	24.2	26.8
Foreign	...	4.7	4.8	...	8.1	-0.4	-0.2	-0.1	0.0	0.0	-1.1	2.6	7.8	4.9	4.2	3.5
Grants	...	4.7	4.8	...	4.1	...	...	...	0.0	0.0	0.0	1.5	3.3	0.4	0.3	0.3
Domestic	...	...	0.0	35.1	14.7	36.2	18.0	33.4	26.6	15.7	11.4	7.2	12.7	13.6	20.0	23.4
Banking system	...	...	0.0	35.1	11.8	31.0	12.6	28.5	22.7	4.4	11.1	5.7	8.1	5.6	14.4	17.2
Banque du Liban	...	...	0.2	19.6	4.9	2.9	-7.5	9.9	16.9	-10.3	-7.0	-0.9	-10.1	-0.2	-5.9	11.8
Commercial banks	...	...	-0.2	15.5	6.9	28.1	20.0	18.5	5.8	14.7	18.1	6.6	18.2	5.7	20.3	5.4
Nonbank private	...	...	...	...	2.9	5.2	5.4	4.9	3.9	11.3	0.3	1.5	4.5	8.1	5.7	6.2

Sources: Ministry of Finance; Banque du Liban (BdL); Council for Development and Reconstruction (CDR); IMF staff estimates.

[1]Includes the treasury and the foreign and domestically financed CDR capital expenditure. Excludes other public entities except for budgetary transfers. See Table A6 in the Statistical Appendix for details of public finance data.

thorities' attempt to maintain a minimum of public services and social services—for example, through subsidies on various commodities and services or through transfers, higher military expenditures, and increased interest payments. As a result, sizable budget deficits emerged, which were to a significant extent financed by the central bank. At the end of the war, public finances and their administration were in a state of disarray: the administrative infrastructure of the ministry of finance was reduced to a bare minimum; the revenue structure was unbalanced in its reliance on a few indirect tax and nontax revenue sources; existing taxes were complicated and diffi-

cult to administer; and the newly formed government inherited a substantial amount of public debt (the net public debt amounted to 87 percent of GDP at the end of 1990).

Postwar Normalization, 1991–92

After the reestablishment of a government of national unity at the end of 1990, the fiscal situation in 1991 and 1992 improved markedly for several reasons (Figure 3.2). First, revenue recovered as the government regained control over revenue sources, particularly with respect to customs revenue and

Figure 3.2. Public Finances

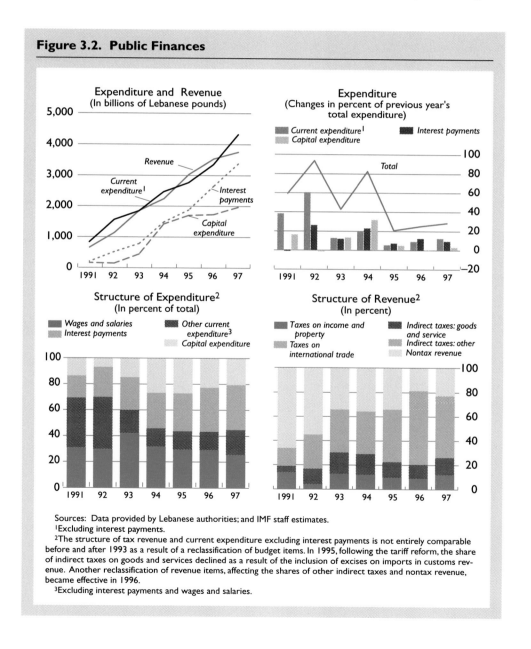

Sources: Data provided by Lebanese authorities; and IMF staff estimates.
[1]Excluding interest payments.
[2]The structure of tax revenue and current expenditure excluding interest payments is not entirely comparable before and after 1993 as a result of a reclassification of budget items. In 1995, following the tariff reform, the share of indirect taxes on goods and services declined as a result of the inclusion of excises on imports in customs revenue. Another reclassification of revenue items, affecting the shares of other indirect taxes and nontax revenue, became effective in 1996.
[3]Excluding interest payments and wages and salaries.

nontax revenue. Second, the rapid growth resulting from the normalization of economic activity reinforced the revenue increase. Third, the elimination of war-related expenditures and an expenditure restraint (including a hiring freeze) led to a decline of expenditure in terms of GDP. As a result, the overall fiscal deficit, as a percent of GDP, dropped from 30 percent in 1990 to 13 percent in 1991 and to 11 percent in 1992.

Revenue Developments and Policies, 1993–97

In contrast with the period 1991–92, during which revenue increases were primarily the result of the reestablished government authority over revenue sources and the normalization of economic activity, the authorities embarked on a number of reforms to mobilize revenue during the period 1993–97. Reflecting the favorable revenue effects of major reforms introduced during this period and the improvement in the tax administration, Lebanon's tax ratio (total tax revenue as a percentage of GDP) increased from 5.4 percent in 1992 to 12.6 percent in 1997 (Table 3.2), and tax revenue registered a buoyancy ratio of 1.8 during 1993–97. The principal reform measures included the following steps.

Duties and taxes on imports. This category of taxes for the period 1993–97 registered the highest buoyancy ratio, 2.2, reflecting the favorable revenue

effects of the 1995 tariff reform and the temporary increase in imports required for reconstruction. The reform measures included the introduction of a minimum tariff rate of 2 percent, the reduction of the number of tariff rates and the number of tariff lines, the consolidation of various taxes collected by different ministries at the customs into a single, unified tariff, and the inclusion of excise taxes on imported goods in the tariff. They also included the elimination of the so-called customs exchange rate for valuation purposes, which was overvalued compared with market exchange rates.[3] Following these reforms, customs revenues in nominal terms almost doubled between 1994 and 1995, despite the relative decline of the share of imports in GDP. However, the inclusion of excises and various other taxes and fees in the tariff has led to some decline in revenue from taxes on goods and services and nontax revenue. Therefore, the overall revenue effect should be assessed using overall tax revenue rather than customs revenue alone.

---

[3]The adjustment of the customs valuation exchange rate to prevailing market rates was combined with a proportional reduction in tariff rates. At the time of the adjustment, the net revenue effect of the two measures was zero. Over time, however, the introduction of a market-based customs valuation exchange rate has ensured that customs revenue will not be eroded by inflation.

Table 3.2. Revenue in Percent of GDP and Buoyancies of Major Categories of Taxes and Other Revenue[1]

| | 1993 | 1994 | 1995 | 1996 | 1997 | Buoyancy | | |
						1993–95	1993–96	1993–97
				(In percent of GDP)				
Taxes on income, profits, and property	1.8	1.8	1.6	1.6	2.0	0.7	0.7	1.3
Taxes on goods and services[2]	2.5	2.5	2.1	2.0	2.3	0.5	0.4	1.0
Duties and taxes on imports[2]	5.0	5.2	7.3	8.0	7.5	2.7	2.6	2.2
In percent of imports	9.1	9.3	13.2	14.4	...	3.6	5.3	...
Other taxes[3]	...	...	...	2.5	0.8	...	...	...
Total tax revenue	9.3	9.4	11.1	14.0	12.6	1.7	2.4	1.8
Nontax revenue[3]	4.8	5.2	5.7	3.3	3.8	1.7	0.1	0.5
Total revenue	14.1	14.6	16.8	17.3	16.4	1.8	1.6	1.4

Sources: Ministry of Finance; and IMF staff calculations.
[1]See Table A6 in the Statistical Appendix for details of the revenue data.
[2]With the 1995 tariff reform, the principal excise and some other taxes on goods and services became part of customs duties and are recorded in duties and taxes on imports.
[3]Under the revised budget classification scheme of 1996, some revenue, such as fiscal stamp duties, which were classified as nontax revenue until 1995, are now included in the new item "other taxes."

Taxes on income and profits. This tax category, despite some progression in nominal rates, registered a buoyancy ratio of less than unity until 1996, reflecting the major income tax reform of 1993. The reform included the following measures: (1) the reduction in the nominal tax rates from 26 percent to 10 percent on corporate profits and from 15 percent to 5 percent on dividends and on other corporate distributions; (2) the reduction of the top marginal rates of individual income taxes from 32 percent to 10 percent for wages and salaries, and from 50 percent to 10 percent for individual business profits; (3) the adoption of an amnesty program that added 9,700 taxpayers; and (4) accelerating the payment of taxes withheld at the source by having the withholders release the funds quarterly (before the reform, these taxes were paid by withholders at the time of filing the declaration). The reduction of the nominal tax rates was intended to encourage the flow of international capital and direct investments and improve the voluntary compliance by taxpayers. In 1997, after significant strengthening of the tax administration, the revenue yield of their tax category improved and the buoyancy ratio reached a value of 1.3.

Taxes on goods and services. During the period 1993–95, the excise rates on tobacco and cigarettes were raised from 5 percent to 30 percent, and the prices of petroleum products were also raised a number of times to narrow the gap with the international prices. The taxation of real estate transactions also yielded increasing revenue given the real estate boom of 1993–95. Despite these developments, this category of taxes registered the lowest buoyancy ratio (1.0) during the period 1993–97. This can be attributed to the collection of principal excises at the stage of importing and recording of their revenue with that from customs duties, as explained earlier.

Analyzing the evolution of the structure of revenue over the period 1993–97 shows that the improvements in the tax revenue mobilization are primarily the result of the customs reform of 1995 (Figure 3.2). The decline in the share of taxes on income and profits until 1996 reflected the combination of the revenue effects of the 1993 reform and weaknesses in taxpayer compliance and tax collection (see below). The reform of income taxation has therefore not yet resulted in the expected increased yield even with the improvements registered in 1997. Today, Lebanon's revenue structure is unbalanced, as it is relying heavily on three sources: imports, some excisable goods, and a plethora of taxable public services and administrative fees. Most domestic transactions and a large part of income are not effectively subject to taxation.

The ministry of finance recognizes the need to enhance its administrative capacity and has embarked on an ambitious project of modernizing and comput-

erizing the budget process and revenue administration. Regarding the latter, the creation of a database on taxpayers, particularly for taxes on income and profits, has been of utmost importance.[4] The modernization project in the ministry's revenue department has included a countrywide campaign to enforce taxpayer registration, the buildup of auditing capacity and expertise, and the streamlining and automatization of tax administration procedures. These measures have the potential to increase substantially the yield of revenue from taxes on income and profits over the next few years.

Expenditure Developments and Policies, 1993–97

A sharp increase in government expenditure has been the predominant characteristic of public finances during the period 1993–97. Government expenditure rose from 23 percent of GDP in 1993 to 42 percent in 1997 (Figure 3.2 and Table 3.1), with all expenditure categories, albeit to a different degree, contributing to the increase.

Current expenditure (excluding interest payments). This expenditure category consists primarily of salaries and wages, purchases of goods and services, and transfers and subsidies. The government has, in general, succeeded in containing the overall wage bill through wage freezes despite considerable political pressure to compensate government employees for the accumulated loss of purchasing power on wages during and after the civil war. In late 1995, a retroactive wage increase was granted (from January 1, 1995 onward).[5] On a cash basis, only one-third of the retroactive increase was effectively disbursed in 1995; the full effect of the wage increase only materialized in 1996. Since then, the government has adopted the policy that further wage increases will only be granted if they are covered by compensating revenue measures. Subsidies to public enterprises have remained important, reflecting the slow cost-recovery capability experienced by providers of basic public services. The ongoing conflict with Israel has also led to recurrent transfers to people and institutions in the south of Lebanon.

Interest payments. Interest payments have been a major factor underlying the growth dynamics of ex-

---

[4]Prewar taxpayer records are outdated, and the gap between registered and potential taxpayers has become large. It is estimated that less than half of all households and firms that would have to file for income and profit taxes under current tax laws are registered. Moreover, about 95 percent of all income and profit tax revenue in 1996 and before was based on declared income only as the auditing and administrative capacity of the revenue department at the ministry of finance was limited.

[5]For the lowest wage categories, the increase amounted to 20 percent. Middle- and upper-wage categories received increases between 10 percent and 20 percent.

penditure. Since 1991, the deficit has been financed almost entirely by issuing debt, largely denominated in domestic currency, to institutions and agents other than the central bank. In the context of the government's exchange-rate-based nominal anchor policy, and given the significant domestic and regional political risks, nominal interest rates on domestic currency assets have been high and subject to dramatic adjustments. Together with the rapid accumulation of public debt, this has led to sharp increases in budgetary interest payments.

Capital expenditure. After the launch of the Horizon 2000 program, the government embarked on a large number of infrastructure rehabilitation and enhancement projects, and capital expenditure rose from 3.4 percent of GDP in 1993 to 9.3 percent in 1994 and 9.4 percent in 1995. In the preparation of the program, the government had envisaged spreading the capital expenditure in nominal terms equally across the 12-year planning period. Capital expenditure as a percentage of GDP would therefore decline over time, leading to some built-in fiscal adjustment. This effect was already visible in 1996 and 1997, when with almost unchanged levels in nominal terms, capital expenditure fell to 8.5 and 8.6 percent of GDP, respectively.

Fiscal Policies and Public Debt Dynamics, 1990–97

Since 1991, large budget deficits have been largely financed through issuing debt, particularly in the form of short-term treasury bills denominated in Lebanese pounds. During 1991–93, the ratio of net public debt to GDP decreased despite very sizable primary deficits and the nominal depreciation of the Lebanese pound on account of the rapid growth and the negative real interest rates on the public debt (Table 3.3, Figure 3.3).[6] The negative real interest rates were associated with the substantial inflation during 1991–93 and the favorable financial market sentiments after the appointment of Prime Minister Hariri in the fall of 1992. In 1994, the restrictive monetary policy stance implied by the exchange-rate-based nominal anchor policy led to a single-digit inflation rate and real interest rates on the public debt turned positive. Moreover, political uncertainties

were associated with pressures on the exchange rate peg, and the central bank had to increase domestic interest rates to prevent excessive reserve losses. Accordingly, the favorable interest rate dynamics reversed, and net public debt started to grow. From a low of 38 percent of GDP at the end of 1993, it increased to an estimated 97 percent of GDP at the end of 1997. Given the persistent primary deficits and the high interest rates, Lebanon's fiscal situation has raised concern about the sustainability of the public debt dynamics.

Fiscal Adjustment and the 1998 Budget

In light of the large deviations of the actual budget deficits and the actual debt path from targets that had been registered from 1994 onward, the Lebanese government began recognizing the need for additional fiscal adjustment beyond the measures described above. In 1996 and 1997, the fiscal adjustment was mainly underpinned by expenditure restraint and increased revenues resulting from economic growth and improved tax administration (Table 3.4). This strategy proved to be unsuccessful, however. Expenditure restraint was difficult, partly because of the large accumulated carryovers in capital expenditure approved in previous budgets. Once approved, these expenditures could be spent at any time and were difficult to control. Similarly, given the debt and interest rate dynamics, interest payments also turned out to be difficult to predict and control. Revenue as a percent of GDP improved but not enough to meet the ambitious budget targets. The problems associated with controlling the fiscal situation became obvious during 1997, when the annual deficit target in nominal terms was almost reached by the end of July. To contain the deviation from budgetary targets for the remainder of 1997, the authorities enacted a number of revenue measures: excise duties on automobiles were increased in July; the government's share of revenues collected from cellular phone calls was increased effective August 1; and customs duties and prices on tobacco products were increased in August. These measures are estimated to have generated revenues amounting to LL 250 billion on an annual basis (1.1 percent of GDP) and close to LL 100 billion in 1997 (0.4 percent of GDP).

In the preparation for the 1998 budget, the government decided to address the fiscal problems more forcefully by relying on both revenue and expenditure measures. The overall target was to initiate front-loaded fiscal adjustment that would make a significant contribution to stabilizing the debt dynamics. On the revenue side, the budget incorpo-

---

[6]Throughout the section, the concept of net public debt is used. Net public debt is defined as total public debt minus government deposits with the banking system. The latter have emerged, beyond normal levels implied by seasonal revenue fluctuations, as a result of sterilization operations of the central bank that served both monetary policy and debt management purposes (see Section V). While these operations imply quasi-fiscal costs given the positive interest rate differential with respect to foreign currency assets, they do not create any net debt liabilities for the treasury and are therefore ignored here.

Table 3.3. Public Debt and Public Debt Dynamics[1]

	1990	1991	1992	1993	1994	1995	1996	1997
				(In percent of GDP)				
Gross public debt	98.4	66.2	49.0	48.5	69.4	78.1	98.9	102.7
Domestic	75.2	54.0	44.0	44.2	61.1	66.5	84.4	86.5
External	23.2	12.3	5.3	4.3	8.3	11.5	14.1	16.2
Government deposits	11.5	8.0	10.9	10.6	17.2	15.0	19.0	6.1
Net public debt	86.9	58.3	38.1	37.9	52.2	63.1	79.9	96.6
Discounted net public debt[2]	...	...	...	...	47.5	55.5	65.0	75.8
Change in net public debt	...	−28.6	−20.2	−0.2	14.2	10.9	16.9	17.0
Contribution of:[3]								
Primary deficit	...	8.1	5.9	3.3	10.8	8.0	7.6	11.1
Domestic interest factor	...	−35.0	−26.1	−5.5	4.9	2.1	5.0	5.9
External interest factor	...	−12.1	−6.3	−1.1	−0.5	−0.5	−0.4	−0.8
Exchange rate valuation	...	0.5	5.8	−0.2	−0.1	−0.2	−0.3	−0.2
Discrepancy	...	9.9	0.4	3.5	−0.8	1.6	4.7	1.1
Memorandum items								
Implied real interest rate on net public debt	...	−38.1	−78.3	−3.0	21.9	12.9	14.4	12.3
Growth adjusted	...	−76.3	−82.8	−10.0	13.9	6.4	10.4	8.3
Implied interest factor on net public debt	...	0.6	0.5	0.9	1.1	1.0	1.1	1.0
Implied interest factor on external debt	...	0.5	0.5	0.8	0.9	0.9	1.0	0.9
Growth factor	...	2.1	2.3	1.4	1.2	1.2	1.1	1.1
Exchange rate factor	...	1.0	2.1	0.9	1.0	1.0	1.0	1.0
Discount factor[2]	...	...	...	...	0.9	0.9	0.8	0.8

Sources: Banque du Liban, various publications: IMF, *International Financial Statistics*; and IMF staff estimates and calculations.

[1]See Table A7 in the Statistical Appendix for details of the public debt.

[2]See footnote 23 in the appendix for details of the calculations.

[3]The decomposition of the changes in the net public debt (as a percent of GDP) in this table and in Figure 3.2 is based on the following identity:

$$b_{t+1} - b_t = pb_t + \left(\frac{r_t - \hat{y}_t}{1 + \hat{y}_t}\right) b_t + \left(\frac{\hat{S}_{t+1}}{(1 + \hat{y}_t)(1 + \pi_t)}\right) f_t + d_t,$$

where b denotes the outstanding net public debt in percent of GDP; pb is the primary balance in percent of GDP; r represents the real interest rate on net government debt; y is real GDP; S stands for the end-of-period nominal exchange rate; f for the foreign currency debt in percent of GDP; π is the inflation rate; d is a discrepancy; t is a time index; and a hat over a variable denotes a percentage change. The second term is referred to as the interest factor in this table and Figure 3.2, while the third term is the exchange rate valuation factor. The discrepancy arises as a result of including accrued interest in the data on outstanding long-term public debt, a significant share of treasury bills in total public debt, cash accounting of interest payments in the budget, the exchange rate valuation of foreign currency related debt flows during the year, and deficiencies in the recording of expenditure by public institutions not included in the central government budget. The real interest rate on the public debt in period t is calculated as the ratio of interest payment in period t over the end-of-period stock of net debt in period $t-1$ minus the current period inflation rate.

rated a 2 percentage point increase in import duties on virtually all imports and a new 5 percent service tax on hotels and restaurants; both measures are seen as a first step to the introduction of a general sales tax (GST). Other revenue measures included (1) the simplification of and increases in road-user taxes; (2) increases in the yearly tax on private cargo trucks and the cement tax; (3) the introduction of or increases in other fees and charges (on residence permits, passport issuance and deed renewal). On the expenditure side, the budget envisaged reducing the number of school teachers and professors,[7] as well as contractual employees in the ministry of informa-

tion, while increasing the overall expenditure on social sectors; incorporated a provision to cancel all uncommitted carryover from the year 1995 and earlier; and included for the first time in the budget presentation all nonbudget treasury expenditures to ensure that actual cash outlays would be in line with budget projections. These measures, taking into account the envisaged capital expenditures and interest payments on public debt are projected to reduce the overall budget deficit to about 15 percent of GDP and the primary deficit to about 2.2 percent of GDP.

The budgetary outcomes for the first half of 1998 confirm the government's more determined efforts to achieve fiscal adjustment. In terms of expenditure, the overall budget balance during January–June 1998 amounted to 35 percent, well below the out-

---

[7]The reduction was intended to reduce over-staffing and was not expected to affect the quality of services delivered.

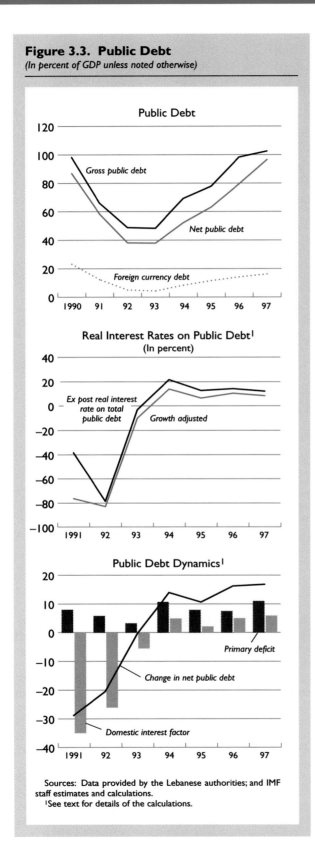

Figure 3.3. Public Debt
(In percent of GDP unless noted otherwise)

Public Debt

Gross public debt

Net public debt

Foreign currency debt

Real Interest Rates on Public Debt[1]
(In percent)

Ex post real interest rate on total public debt

Growth adjusted

Public Debt Dynamics[1]

Primary deficit

Change in net public debt

Domestic interest factor

Sources: Data provided by the Lebanese authorities; and IMF staff estimates and calculations.
[1]See text for details of the calculations.

comes observed in 1996 and 1997.[8] Moreover, excluding foreign-financed capital expenditure, the primary balance was positive, implying some repayment of net domestic public debt. In April 1998, the government enacted further revenue increases in anticipation of a forthcoming wage increase effective in the beginning of 1999. This wage increase had been agreed upon in March after government wages had been frozen since the beginning of 1996. Despite strong political pressures for an immediate increase, the increase was delayed, and any retroactivity was made conditional on further revenue measures beyond those enacted in April. Compensatory revenue measures put into effect at the end of April included a 2 percentage point increase in tariffs on all imports and a 10 percentage point increase in taxes on cigarettes and tobacco. These increases provided further guarantees for the 1998 budget targets to be met.

Theoretical Aspects of Fiscal Sustainability

Overall, the fiscal adjustment envisaged by the government aims at achieving fiscal sustainability. In the remainder of this section, the government's adjustment plans are reviewed in light of this notion. According to Razin (1996), a fiscal policy program is considered to be sustainable if it meets the solvency requirements,[9] can be continued into the indefinite future, is consistent with high and sustained medium-term economic growth, and is not prone to an abrupt and discrete change when the economy is hit by a shock. In terms of instruments, the issue is the level and structure of adjustment in expenditure and revenue needed to ensure that a fiscal policy program becomes sustainable.

From this perspective, the sustainability of a fiscal policy program depends, among other factors, on the overall macroeconomic policy mix, the current level and structure of expenditure and revenue, and the current level and structure of the debt-to-GDP ratio. Ideally, the degree of adjustment needed to ensure the sustainability of fiscal policies should be evaluated on the basis of a comprehensive macroecono-

---

[8]In their budget presentation and monthly reporting, the Lebanese authorities do not include foreign financed capital expenditure, that is, capital expenditure that is directly financed by nonresidents in the context of the reconstruction program. To allow for a comparison, the format of the budget presentiation in Table 3.4 excludes this expenditure category but it is included in all other fiscal tables presented in this paper.

[9]Solvency requires that the sum of the expected present value of all present and future expenditure and the current level of debt has to be equal to the net present value of current and future revenue. The solvency concept and its implications for fiscal sustainability are discussed in the appendix.

Table 3.4. Budget Targets and Actuals[1]
(In billions of Lebanese pounds)

	1996			1997			1998	
	Budget	Actuals	Jan.–June[2]	Budget	Actuals	Jan.–June	Budget	Jan.–June
Revenue	4,022	3,534	1,630	4,100	3,753	1,797	4,600	2,293
Of which: customs duties	1,800	1,632	769	1,800	1,722	773	2,190	977
Expenditure	6,458	7,225	2,989	6,433	9,162	3,683	7,920	3,528
Of which: interest expenditure	2,250	2,468	797	2,700	3,378	1,558	3,200	1,583
Overall balance[3]	−2,436	−3,691	−1,359	−2,333	−5,409	−187	−3,320	−1,235
Primary balance[4]	−186	−1,223	−562	367	−2,031	−329	−120	348
Memorandum items								
Overall balance[3]								
In percent of expenditure	−37.7	−51.1	−45.5	−36.3	−59.0	−51.2	−41.9	−35.0
In percent of GDP	−11.5	−18.1	...	−9.8	−23.6	...	−12.8	...
GDP	21,122	20,417	...	23,840	22,878	...	25,946	...

Sources: Ministry of Finance; Banque du Liban.

[1]Includes the treasury and the domestically financed capital expenditure by the Council for Development and Reconstruction (CDR). Foreign financed CDR expenditures are excluded to faciliate the comparison with monthly data published by the authorities. See Table A6 in the Statistical Appendix for details of public finance data.

[2]Cumulation based on monthly data.

[3]Excluding foreign grants.

[4]Excluding foreign financed capital expenditures.

metric model. For Lebanon, as for many others, such models are not available, and a simpler approach is needed. To evaluate the level and structure of Lebanon's fiscal adjustment need, two steps are proposed: first, assess the level of the adjustment needed to stabilize the debt dynamics; second, ascertain the structure of adjustment needed in expenditure and revenue.

The Level of Adjustment Needed to Stabilize the Debt Dynamics

When assessing of the level of adjustment needed to stabilize the debt dynamics, so-called primary gap measures are useful tools.[10] The T-period primary gap is defined as the difference between the current primary deficit and the average annual primary balance needed to achieve a certain target debt-to-GDP ratio $\bar{b}$ in T years ahead. A positive primary gap implies that the primary balance needs to be increased to achieve the debt target. If the current primary balance pb is assumed to remain constant throughout the period t to $t+T$, the T-period primary gap GAP^T is defined as:[11]

$$GAP^T(b) = \frac{\left[(1 + r_t^g) b_t - \prod_{v=t}^{T} \frac{1}{1 + r_v^g} \bar{b}\right]}{\prod_{s=t}^{T} \prod_{v=t}^{s} \frac{1}{1 + r_v^g}} - pb_t, \quad (1)$$

where r^g denotes the growth adjusted real interest rate, b is the debt-to-GDP ratio, and t stands for a time index.[12] The intuition underlying the gap-formula in equation (1) is as follows: The first term on the right hand side captures the difference between the current debt-to-GDP ratio and the net present value of the target value of the debt-to-GDP ratio on an annual basis. The difference is the annual value for the primary balance needed to achieve the debt target. The second term provides the net present value of the current primary balance, which is assumed to prevail throughout period t to T, also on an annual basis. The first term minus the second term in equation (1) then equals the gap, that is, the difference between the average primary balance needed and the planned primary balance. If the primary balance under current policies is not constant

---

[10]See Blanchard (1990) and Buiter (1997) for a detailed discussion.

[11]The following exposition abstracts from valuation problems associated with foreign currency debt, given the forward-looking

perspective. Table 3.3 shows that, with the exception of 1992, valuation changes have not contributed much to debt dynamics in the recent past.

[12]The growth-adjusted real interest rate is defined as $r^g = (1 + r)/(1 + \hat{y}) - 1$, where $\hat{y}$ denotes the growth rate of real GDP.

during the period t to T, the gap measure has to be rewritten as:

$$GAP^T(\bar{b}) = \left[(1 + r_t^g) b_t - \prod_{v=t}^{T} \frac{1}{1 + r_v^g} \bar{b}\right] / $$
$$\left| \sum_{s=t}^{T} \prod_{v=t}^{s} \frac{1}{1 + r_v^g} - \sum_{s=t}^{T} \prod_{v=t}^{s} \frac{1}{1 + r_v^g} pb_s \right| $$
$$\sum_{s=t}^{T} \prod_{v=t}^{s} \frac{1}{1 + r_v^g}. \qquad (2)$$

In practice, fiscal consolidation tends to be gradual since administrative, economic and political factors constrain the adjustment that can be achieved on a year-by-year basis. If such a gradual adjustment in the primary balance could be incorporated in the primary gap measures, the latter would provide a useful benchmark for assessing actual medium-term fiscal adjustment plans. Assuming a typical, smooth adjustment path, the gradual convergence of the primary balance to its medium-term target $\overline{pb}$ can be modeled as a first-order autoregressive (AR(1)) process:

$$pb_t - \overline{pb} = \rho (pb_{t-1} - \overline{pb}), \quad 1 > \rho > 0, \qquad (3)$$

where ρ is a measure for speed of the gradual adjustment. The speed with which the primary balance approaches its targeted medium-term level is inversely related to the coefficient ρ. In this case, the primary gap would be defined as:

$$GAP^T(\bar{b}, \overline{pb}, \rho) = \left[(1 + r_t^g) b_t - \prod_{v=t}^{T} \frac{1}{1 + r_v^g} \bar{b}\right] / $$
$$\left| \sum_{s=t}^{T} \prod_{v=t}^{s} \frac{1}{1 + r_v^g} - \overline{pb} - (pb_t - \overline{pb}) \sum_{s=t}^{T} \prod_{v=t}^{s} \frac{1}{1 + r_v^g} \rho^{s-t} \right| $$
$$\sum_{s=t}^{T} \prod_{v=t}^{s} \frac{1}{1 + r_v^g}. \qquad (4)$$

The application of primary gap measures is typically a difficult undertaking since data on variables, which are linked through various channels, are required for an analysis based on empirically validated relationships. For example, the growth-adjusted real interest rate, the debt-to-GDP ratio, and the fiscal adjustment path are all linked through the crowding out mechanism: An increase in the debt-to-GDP ratio leads, ceteris paribus, to an increased absorption of private savings, which requires higher real interest rates for the bond market to clear. This increase in real interest rates decreases the medium-term growth rate through its negative impact on investment, which, in turn, reduces the growth path of the capital stock and thus potential output.[13] Any implementa-

tion of primary gap measures should take these channels into account. It is exactly at this stage that a fully specified macroeconometric model would be useful.

In the absence of such a model, a simpler approach is required. Frequently, a constant growth-adjusted real interest rate is used. Some authors have used a parameterized interest rate function, which relates the real interest rate to the debt-to-GDP ratio.[14] The latter approach is associated with considerable uncertainty, given that econometric estimates of the relationship between real interest rates and the level of government debt provide, at best, reduced-form parameters. If one is interested, for policy analysis, in determining a path for the primary balance that would allow a country to reach a certain target debt-to-GDP ratio, the application of constant growth-adjusted real interest rates based on historical averages or a priori limits, or both, based on the experience of other countries appear preferable.

Another difficulty arising in this context is the choice of the target debt-to-GDP ratio. Theoretical considerations suggest to opt for a low ratio in light of the crowding out mechanism. Moreover, lower values for the debt-to-GDP ratio facilitate the macroeconomic management in general since they reduce the problems associated with the refinancing of maturing debt and the incentives to reduce the real value of the government debt through surprise inflation. The experience of many countries suggests that debt-to-GDP ratios above 100 percent to 120 percent of GDP can lead to difficulties in macroeconomic policy management if they are maintained over a long period.[15]

The Structure of the Adjustment

Achieving a sustainable fiscal policy program typically involves adjustments not only in the level of the primary deficit but also in the structure of expenditure and revenue. The latter are often the result of the expenditure and revenue measures enacted to reduce the fiscal imbalance. In general, these measures should aim at increasing government saving, reducing expenditure for services that can be provided by the private sector or which are unproductive, better targeting of recipients of transfers and subsidies, and minimizing the distortionary effects of taxes.

Regarding expenditure adjustments, recent research on fiscal policy and growth has provided some

---

[13]The strength of these effects depends on whether Ricardian equivalence holds. At the limit, under conditions of full Ricardian equivalence, they would be nonexistent. See Barro (1974) and Bernheim (1987), among others, on this issue.

[14]See Ford and Laxton (1995), Helbling and Wescott (1995), Mongelli (1996), and Tanzi and Fanizza (1995), among others, on the relationship between real interest rates and government debt. In all these studies, the real interest rate rather than the growth-adjusted real interest rate is used as a dependent variable.

[15]See, for example, Dornbusch and Draghi (1990) and Obstfeld (1994).

indications on expenditure components that tend to support growth. On the expenditure side, adjustment should be such that government expenditures that are essential for enhancing growth are preserved at their optimal level.[16] These expenditures include capital expenditure and expenditure on health and education, all of which contribute to the accumulation of physical and human capital. Unfortunately, the optimal level of these expenditures is difficult to ascertain for two reasons. First, it depends on the specific structures of the growth model used, in particular the specification of the production function.[17] Second, reliable empirical estimates for key parameters of aggregate production and consumption functions are often not available. Moreover, the optimal expenditure level is also a function of the tax system if taxation has distortionary effects. A reconstruction economy faces not only the problem of determining the optimal level of infrastructure capital, but also that of the optimal convergence to this level from a public capital stock destroyed by war. The determination of the optimal adjustment path is subject to caveats that are similar to those regarding the optimal level. However, from a perspective of maximizing long-run growth, standard "turnpike" considerations suggest that it would be optimal to move to the long-run equilibrium level of the capital stock as fast as possible. In the end, it is likely that macroeconomic policy constraints, fiscal sustainability considerations, and the project implementation capacity will determine the path of capital and other growth-enhancing expenditure during a reconstruction.

Concerning revenue, recent research has recommended adjustments in revenue structure such that the yield on taxes is constant or increasing with GDP growth to allow for tax smoothing. Moreover, the tax system should be balanced so that tax revenue is not overly dependent on one source. In this way, the system is less prone to shocks to the tax base of a particular tax category. Recent research on fiscal policy and growth has also emphasized the role of broad-based consumption taxes as a means to raise revenue without imposing excessive distortions on an economy.

Fiscal Adjustment and Aspects of Fiscal Sustainability

With the 1998 budget, the government has made determined efforts to embark on a front-loaded fiscal adjustment program that aims at ensuring medium-term fiscal sustainability. As discussed above, a program aiming at fiscal sustainability should be reviewed in the light of two fundamental questions. First, is the envisaged adjustment in the primary deficit sufficiently large to ensure that the debt dynamics is consistent with solvency and medium-term macroeconomic stability? Second, is the adjustment in the structure of expenditure and revenue consistent with growth and reducing their vulnerability to exogenous shocks and structural changes in the economy?

The Adjustment Need Implied by Primary Gap Measures

The computation of primary gap measures for Lebanon is difficult because some of the basic macroeconomic relationships needed in the calculation of empirically based gaps cannot be estimated because of missing data or structural breaks, or both. For this reason, two sets of a priori primary gap measures, for different values of the growth-adjusted real interest rate and the target debt-to-GDP ratio, are computed. The first set comprises 10-year primary gap measures (Table 3.5, left panel). The 10-year primary gap is the difference between the average, annual primary balance needed to reach a target net debt-to-GDP ratio at the end of year 10 and the current primary deficit, that is, 11.1 percent of GDP in 1997. The second set consists of 15-year primary gap measures, which are also based on the 1997 primary deficit of 11.1 percent of GDP (Table 3.5, right panel). For the growth-adjusted real interest rates, values of −5 percent to 10 percent were selected. While standard economic theory suggests that the growth-adjusted real interest rate is strictly positive in the long run, the possibility that it is close to zero or even negative during a sharp growth acceleration at some phases of reconstruction cannot be excluded. For the target net-debt-to-GDP ratio, values ranging from 60 percent—the Maastricht criteria— to 150 percent, which certainly is an upper limit to a debt-to-GDP ratio that is sustainable in the medium term are used in the calculations.

For the understanding of the implications of the primary gaps, it is useful to start with the case of 95 percent, that is, a stabilization of the net debt around the end-of-1997 level. The 10-year primary gap at a zero growth-adjusted real interest rate amounts to 9.5 percent. Hence, a stabilization of the debt dynamics at the current level requires achieving a primary deficit of about 1.6 percent of GDP over the entire 10 years provided that the interest cost of the debt grows in line with GDP. However, if the real interest rate exceeds the growth rate of GDP by a margin of 5 percentage points, additional adjustment of

---

[16]Tanzi and Zee (1996) discuss the linkages between the budgetary structure and long-run growth from the perspective of both recent empirical and theoretical research.

[17]See Barro and Sala-i-Martin (1992, 1995) on public-finance-related aspects of growth.

Table 3.5. Primary Gap Measures[1]
(In percent of GDP)

Target Net Debt-to-GDP Ratio	Ten-Year Primary Gaps Growth-adjusted real interest rate (in percent)				Fifteen-Year Primary Gaps Growth-adjusted real interest rate (in percent)			
	−5	0	5	10	−5	0	5	10
60	5.7	9.5	13.6	18.0	5.2	8.9	12.8	17.2
65	5.1	9.0	13.2	17.7	4.8	8.5	12.6	17.0
70	4.5	8.5	12.8	17.4	4.3	8.2	12.4	16.9
75	3.9	8.0	12.4	17.1	3.8	7.9	12.1	16.7
80	3.2	7.5	12.0	16.8	3.4	7.5	11.9	16.6
85	2.6	7.0	11.6	16.5	2.9	7.2	11.7	16.4
90	2.0	6.5	11.2	16.2	2.4	6.9	11.4	16.2
95	1.4	6.0	10.8	15.8	2.0	6.5	11.2	16.1
100	0.7	5.5	10.4	15.5	1.5	6.2	11.0	15.9
105	0.1	5.0	10.0	15.2	1.1	5.9	10.8	15.8
110	−0.5	4.5	9.6	14.9	0.6	5.5	10.5	15.6
115	−1.1	4.0	9.2	14.6	0.1	5.2	10.3	15.5
120	−1.7	3.5	8.8	14.3	−0.3	4.9	10.1	15.3
125	−2.4	3.0	8.4	14.0	−0.8	4.5	9.8	15.1
130	−3.0	2.5	8.1	13.7	−1.3	4.2	9.6	15.0
135	−3.6	2.0	7.7	13.3	−1.7	3.9	9.4	14.8
140	−4.2	1.5	7.3	13.0	−2.2	3.5	9.1	14.7
145	−4.9	1.0	6.9	12.7	−2.7	3.2	8.9	14.5
150	−5.5	0.5	6.5	12.4	−3.1	2.9	8.7	14.4

Source: IMF staff calculations based on data provided by the Lebanese authorities.
[1]See text for details of the calculations, which are based on the primary deficit recorded in 1997.

about 4.8 percentage points of GDP a year is required. In other words, an annual primary surplus of 3.2 percent of GDP over the next 10 years is needed to maintain a stable debt-to-GDP ratio. The 15-year primary gap amounts to 10.0 percent of GDP in the case of a zero growth-adjusted real interest rate, implying a primary deficit of 1.1 percent of GDP to achieve the debt target. With a growth-adjusted real interest rate of 5 percent, however, the 15-year primary gap measure implies that a primary surplus of 3.6 percent of GDP is needed for a debt target of 95 percent of GDP to be realized.

The figures in Table 3.5 show that the primary gaps are positively correlated with the growth-adjusted real interest rate, reflecting the larger interest rate costs of the debt stock. The correlation with the target net-debt-to-GDP ratio is negative because a larger target value relative to the initial value requires less fiscal adjustment. A comparison of the first panel in Table 3.5 with the second panel shows that the correlations for the 10-year primary gap vary more in both dimensions than in the case of the 15-year primary gap. This larger variation is the result of two mechanisms. If the target net-debt-to-GDP is lower than the debt-to-GDP ratio in the initial pe-

riod, the fiscal adjustment required to achieve the lower target within a shorter time span is larger. For a target ratio that is larger than the current ratio, less fiscal adjustment is required within the 10-year time span than within the 15-year time span because the accumulated interest cost of the debt is smaller.

Overall, the primary gap measures shown in Table 3.5 indicate that the primary deficit target in the 1998 budget is not yet consistent with the stabilization of the ratio of net-public debt to GDP at a value close to the end-of-1997 level as long as the growth-adjusted real interest rates remain larger than zero. This result, however, should be interpreted with caution as the primary gap measures analyzed so far are based on the assumption that the adjustment in the primary balance is undertaken in one step and maintained throughout the 10- or 15-year period. Given the dramatic improvement in the primary balance needed in the case of Lebanon, it would be unreasonable to assume that such an adjustment could be undertaken in one step. A gradual primary balance adjustment as described by the autoregressive process in equation (3), however, could be feasible in light of the discussion of expenditure and revenue reforms following below. The computation of primary gap measures according to equation (4), therefore, provides one with useful benchmarks for comparison.

Fifteen-year primary gap measures that already incorporate some fiscal adjustment according to equation (3) indicate additional adjustment needs for some parameters combinations (Table 3.6). To illustrate the adjustment, the time path of the primary balance for a period of 15 years is shown in Figure 3.4 for values of the adjustment coefficient ρ ranging from 0.9 to 0.1 and for a medium-term primary surplus target of 2 percent of GDP. For example, starting from a primary deficit of 11.1 percent in 1997, an adjustment coefficient of 0.7 would imply that a zero primary balance would be reached in 2003 while a coefficient of 0.5 would lead to zero primary balance in 2000. Under the assumptions of a zero growth-adjusted real interest rate and positive medium-term primary surplus targets, the primary gaps reported in Table 3.6 show that ambitious ad-

justment paths, that is, paths that aim at reducing the primary deficit by at least 5 percentage points of GDP in the first year (equivalent to values of ρ of 0.5 or less), are consistent with a target net-debt-to-GDP ratio of 80 percent of GDP. With a 5 percent growth-adjusted real interest rate, the primary gap measures indicate a need for further adjustment to attain the same target debt-to-GDP ratio.

What are the implications of these primary gap measures for Lebanon? In the 1998 budget, the targeted primary deficit amounts to 2.4 percent of GDP with the envisaged front-loaded adjustment. For the years thereafter, the government plans to achieve primary surpluses. This adjustment path implies low values (below 0.4) for the adjustment coefficient ρ discussed above. As evident from Table 3.6, such an adjustment path would be consistent with stabilizing the net public debt at the end-1997 level for growth-adjusted real interest rates in the range from zero to 5 percent.

Table 3.6. Fifteen-Year Primary Gaps with Autoregressive(1)-Adjustment[1]
(In percent of GDP)

AR-Adjustment Coefficient	Target Long-Run Primary Balance										
	−2.0	−1.5	−1.0	−0.5	0.0	0.5	1.0	1.5	2.0	2.5	3.0
Target net-debt-to-GDP ratio: 100 percent; growth-adjusted real interest rate: 0 percent											
0.9	3.9	3.1	2.4	1.6	0.9	0.2	−0.6	−1.3	−2.0	−2.8	−3.5
0.7	0.8	0.2	−0.4	−0.9	−1.5	−2.1	−2.7	−3.3	−3.8	−4.4	−5.0
0.5	−0.1	−0.6	−1.1	−1.7	−2.2	−2.7	−3.3	−3.8	−4.3	−4.9	−5.4
0.3	−0.4	−0.9	−1.5	−2.0	−2.5	−3.0	−3.5	−4.0	−4.5	−5.1	−5.6
0.1	−0.6	−1.1	−1.6	−2.1	−2.6	−3.1	−3.6	−4.2	−4.7	−5.2	−5.7
Target net-debt-to-GDP ratio: 80 percent; growth-adjusted real interest rate: 0 percent											
0.9	6.5	5.8	5.1	4.3	3.6	2.8	2.1	1.4	0.6	−0.1	−0.9
0.7	3.5	2.9	2.3	1.7	1.1	0.6	0.0	−0.6	−1.2	−1.7	−2.3
0.5	2.6	2.1	1.5	1.0	0.5	−0.1	−0.6	−1.1	−1.7	−2.2	−2.7
0.3	2.2	1.7	1.2	0.7	0.2	−0.3	−0.8	−1.4	−1.9	−2.4	−2.9
0.1	2.0	1.5	1.0	0.5	0.0	−0.5	−1.0	−1.5	−2.0	−2.5	−3.0
Target net-debt-to-GDP ratio: 100 percent; growth-adjusted real interest rate: 5 percent											
0.9	8.3	7.6	6.8	6.1	5.3	4.6	3.8	3.1	2.3	1.5	0.8
0.7	5.2	4.6	4.0	3.4	2.8	2.3	1.7	1.1	0.5	−0.1	−0.7
0.5	4.2	3.7	3.2	2.6	2.1	1.5	1.0	0.5	−0.1	−0.6	−1.2
0.3	3.8	3.3	2.8	2.2	1.7	1.2	0.7	0.2	−0.4	−0.9	−1.4
0.1	3.5	3.0	2.5	2.0	1.5	1.0	0.5	0.0	−0.5	−1.0	−1.5
Target net-debt-to-GDP ratio: 80 percent; growth-adjusted real interest rate: 5 percent											
0.9	10.3	9.6	8.8	8.1	7.3	6.6	5.8	5.1	4.3	3.5	2.8
0.7	7.2	6.6	6.0	5.4	4.8	4.3	3.7	3.1	2.5	1.9	1.3
0.5	6.2	5.7	5.2	4.6	4.1	3.5	3.0	2.4	1.9	1.4	0.8
0.3	5.8	5.3	4.8	4.2	3.7	3.2	2.7	2.2	1.6	1.1	0.6
0.1	5.5	5.0	4.5	4.0	3.5	3.0	2.5	2.0	1.5	1.0	0.5

Source: IMF staff calculations based on data provided by the authorities.
[1]See text for details of the calculations, which are based on the primary deficit recorded in 1997.

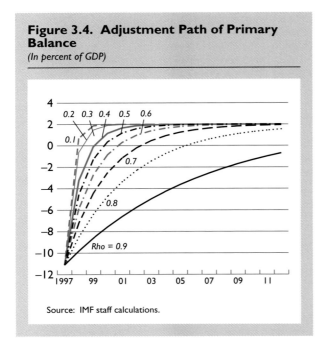

Figure 3.4. Adjustment Path of Primary Balance
(In percent of GDP)

Source: IMF staff calculations.

Adjustments in the Structure of Expenditure and Revenue

There are also issues regarding the structure of expenditure and revenue during fiscal adjustment. For expenditure, the questions are whether capital expenditure can and should be adjusted and whether reductions in other expenditures could contribute to adjustment. For revenue, the questions are whether the current structure is consistent with a constant or even rising yield with respect to GDP growth and what effects the ongoing modernization of the tax administration will have on the revenue yield of income taxes.

Reconstruction and Capital Expenditure

As discussed earlier, government capital expenditure plays an important role in growth. The optimal level of capital expenditure for Lebanon is difficult to determine given the lack of empirical evidence. A cross-country comparison shows that Lebanon's capital expenditure as a percentage of GDP has indeed been high by international standards (Figure 3.5). Over the period 1991–95, the average capital expenditure in a sample of 25 industrial and developing countries amounted to 3.7 percent of GDP (median: 2.7 percent) while that of Lebanon reached 9.1 percent. In a subsample of 16 developing countries, the average level of capital expenditure was about 4.8 percent of GDP over the same period (median: 4.1 percent). A comparison over a longer period (1981–95) yields an average of 4.5 percent of GDP for all countries (median: 3.4 percent), while it was 6.1 percent of GDP for the developing countries in

the sample (median: 4.2 percent).[18] This comparison shows that substantial fiscal adjustment in the order of 3 percent to 5 percent of GDP can be expected from capital expenditure in the medium term once it starts to converge to internationally comparable levels following with the gradual completion of the reconstruction program. In the 1998 budget, a planned decrease in capital expenditure by 2.4 percentage points of GDP contributes indeed to the deficit reduction.

Other Expenditure

The reduction of other expenditure is also difficult, particularly in the short term. In 1997, about 76 percent of current expenditure was accounted for by expenditure that was subject to short-term rigidities: payments for wages and salaries and interest payments. The contribution to fiscal adjustment from these two expenditure items in the medium term depends on progress in fiscal adjustment in the interim (interest payments) and on the pace of civil service reform, which could be a delicate issue in the current sociopolitical environment. While civil service reform could imply substantial short-term costs, its contribution could be substantial in the medium term. In the short term, restraints on the aggregate wage bill could provide important support to fiscal consolidation efforts. Indeed, a newly unchanged nominal aggregate wage bill contributes about 1.2 percentage points of GDP to the overall adjustment. Other current expenditure, including purchases of goods and services for current consumption and transfers (including social spending) account for about 20 percent of expenditure. Reductions in this area could be feasible but are likely to be limited by the need to improve the social safety net and the recurrent expenditure implied by the reconstruction program. Greater private sector participation and cost recovery through user fees (electricity, water) would contribute to reducing the budgetary burden associated with such recurrent expenditure in the future.

Revenue Structure and Modernization of Tax Administration

Lebanon's fiscal consolidation efforts need to involve measures to increase the ratio of revenue to GDP as well as to improve the current revenue structure, which is very dependent on revenue from customs duties as discussed earlier. Currently, most domestically produced goods and services are not

---

[18]This sample was chosen on the basis of data availability. Data on capital expenditure were taken from the IMF's *Government Finance Statistics,* while the nominal GDP data were taken from the IMF's *International Financial Statistics.*

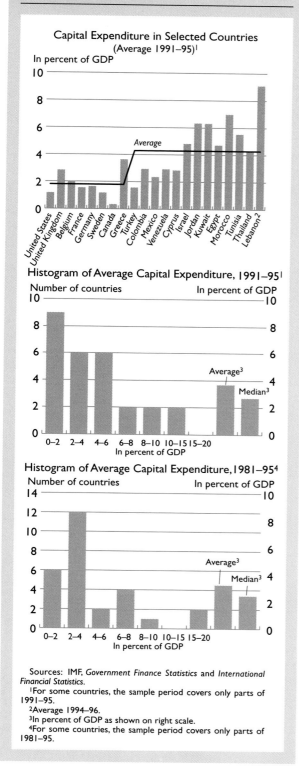

Figure 3.5. Cross-Country Comparison of Capital Expenditure

Capital Expenditure in Selected Countries
(Average 1991–95)[1]

Histogram of Average Capital Expenditure, 1991–95[1]

Histogram of Average Capital Expenditure, 1981–95[4]

Sources: IMF, *Government Finance Statistics* and *International Financial Statistics*.
[1]For some countries, the sample period covers only parts of 1991–95.
[2]Average 1994–96.
[3]In percent of GDP as shown on right scale.
[4]For some countries, the sample period covers only parts of 1981–95.

subject to indirect taxes. Moreover, the ratio of income tax revenue to GDP has been low, and the income tax base has not yet been expanding in line with private sector growth. Therefore, without further revenue measures as a result of the expected structural changes (accelerated growth in domestic production, gradual decline in external imbalances) and shocks, the overall tax revenue, as a percent of GDP, might fall rather than increase in the future

Revenue measures should aim at expanding the tax base to incorporate the most dynamic sectors, on both the demand and income side. On the demand side, a broad-based consumption tax, possibly a general sales tax, could expand the tax base considerably. In 1996, it was estimated that imports amounted to about 50 percent of GDP while private consumption was about 100 percent of GDP. A broad-based consumption tax covering the domestically produced goods and services, therefore, has the potential to almost double the tax base compared with the current base, which only covers the imported part of consumption. Such a tax could also allow the authorities to lower the average import tariff rate and to participate in trade liberalization efforts. On the income side, continued efforts at improving the capacity of the income tax administration and expanding the base of registered taxpayers could also yield additional revenue given the anticipated high private sector growth in the medium term.

Conclusions

In recent years, Lebanon's sizable budget deficits and its large and growing public debt have raised the issue of fiscal sustainability. Rough calculations using primary gap measures based on the 1997 fiscal outcome confirm a need for substantial fiscal adjustment in the medium term to stabilize the ratio of public debt to GDP at levels consistent with macroeconomic and financial stability. If the debt-to-GDP ratio is to be maintained at current levels or to be reduced over the medium term, surpluses in the primary budget balance would have to be run over the years to come. The size of the surpluses critically depends on the growth-adjusted real interest rate. A high GDP growth rate would facilitate the task of fiscal adjustment considerably since the growth-adjusted real interest rate is quite likely to be inversely related to GDP growth.

The timing of fiscal consolidation should be such that front-loaded fiscal adjustment is achieved as further delay would only increase the adjustment need in the future. The 1998 budget target is indeed aimed at converging to such an adjustment path, as a significant drop in the primary budget deficit is envisaged. In 1999 or 2000, a primary surplus is targeted. Such front-loaded adjustment also has the advantage that it puts less strain on the overall macroeconomic policy mix and is likely to support a decline in growth-adjusted real interest rates as it contributes to the credibility of the planned fiscal policy path.

Fiscal adjustment in Lebanon will have to incorporate efforts to generate additional revenue as (1) further reductions in capital expenditure are likely to materialize only in the medium term, (2) a large share of the current expenditures is either subject to short-term rigidities (e.g., interest expenditure), (3) other current spending (excluding interest payments and wages) is small and its further reduction would entail substantial losses in terms of social spending and infrastructure maintenance, and (4) further increases in the tax buoyancy are unlikely given the recent decline in imports as a share of GDP. Moreover, it would also be advantageous to achieve a more balanced tax structure so as to lower the vulnerability to shocks and avoid distortions.

Further revenue measures, including cost-recovery measures related to public infrastructure services, are also consistent with tax-smoothing considerations. Tax-smoothing principles would suggest that the maturity of the debt issued to finance reconstruction projects should be equal to the lifetime of the project and that taxes for the debt service should be levied during the entire lifetime of the project. Accordingly, some cost recovery through taxation or levy of user fees, or both, should already be carried out in the beginning of reconstruction.

Revenue measures could focus on two areas. First, a general sales tax and the extension of excises levied on imports to domestically produced goods would ensure that the yield of taxes on goods and services would be linked to the expected acceleration in the domestic production of goods and services. Second, continued efforts in strengthening the tax administration and the database on registered taxpayers would help increase the returns from taxes on income and property in the medium term. With the expected accelerated private sector growth, these measures would also contribute to ensuring that the overall tax yield is consistent with future sources of growth in the economy.

Regarding the sequencing of measures, revenue measures should be implemented as soon as possible given the rigidities on the expenditure side discussed above. A tight expenditure stance on the aggregate wage bill and other current noninterest expenditure should support the revenue measures. To ensure the front-loaded adjustment, the revenue measures could include temporary measures, such as a surcharge applied to the least distortionary revenue sources (e.g., on a general sales tax or excises), which would be in effect until the medium-term benefits of a civil ser-

vice reform, the convergence of capital expenditure to their medium-term equilibrium level, and the effects of tax reform would materialize. The recent revenue measures enacted by the government are consistent with these recommendations.

Appendix. Intertemporal Government Budget Constraint and Solvency

The concept of government solvency defines a minimum requirement for sustainability. While it is inappropriate for Lebanon under the current circumstances, the concept is nevertheless useful for understanding the broader concept of fiscal sustainability.[19] In the simplest possible form, its essentials can be summarized as follows.[20] In each period, the government's flow budget constraint implies that under the assumption of pure debt financing the end-of-period public debt is given by:

$$B_{t+1} = E_t - TR_t + (1 + R_t) B_t, \qquad (5)$$

where B denotes the outstanding public debt, TR is government revenue, E represents noninterest government expenditure, R is the nominal interest rate on government liabilities, and t is a time subscript. For the subsequent analysis, it is useful to rewrite the flow constraint in equation (6) in terms of the current period GDP:

$$b_{t+1} = e_t - tr_t + \left(\frac{1 + r_t}{1 + \hat{y}_t} \right) b_t, \qquad (6)$$

where a lowercase letter variable denotes a capital letter variable as a fraction of the current period GDP (except for r, the real interest rate), and $\hat{y}$ the growth rate of real GDP. The intertemporal solvency constraint requires that the flow budget constraint in equation (6) is expected to hold in every period in the future, which leads to the condition:

$$\sum_{s=t}^{\infty} \prod_{v=t}^{s} \frac{1}{1 + r_t^g} \, e_s + (1 + r_t^g) b_t = \sum_{s=t}^{\infty} \prod_{v=t}^{s} \frac{1}{1 + r_v^g} \, tr_s, \quad (7)$$

where r^g denotes the growth-adjusted real interest rate, (that is, $1 + r)/(1 + \hat{y}) - 1$. The sum of the expected present value of all present and future expenditure and the current level of debt has therefore to be equal to the net present value of current and future revenue. The condition in equation (7) can be

---

[19]See Buiter (1985, 1997) and Blanchard (1990) for a more detailed discussion.

[20]This exposition abstracts from valuation problems associated with foreign currency debt. Table 3.3 shows that, with the exception of 1992, valuation changes have not contributed much to the debt dynamics.

rewritten using the primary balance pb rather than expenditure and revenue:

$$(1 + r_t^g)b_t = \sum_{s=t}^{\infty} \prod_{v=t}^{s} \frac{1}{1 + r_v^g} pb_s. \qquad (8)$$

If the growth-adjusted real interest rate is positive on average, as suggested by standard models of economic growth, the condition in equation (8) leads to the familiar requirement that the government has to run primary surpluses in the future if it has some outstanding liabilities today. In the derivation of equations (7) and (8), it was assumed that the so-called transversality condition:

$$\lim_{s \to \infty} b_{t+s+1} \prod_{v=t}^{s} \frac{1}{1 + r_v^g} = 0 \qquad (9)$$

holds. This condition can be interpreted as a limit on the average increase in the debt-to-GDP ratio in the future, which has to be lower than the average growth-adjusted real interest rate.[21] Together, the solvency constraints in equations (7) or (8) and the transversality condition in equation (9) ensure the intertemporal consistency of a fiscal program. They provide the accounting framework for the requirements that the debt is serviced in every period and will eventually be repaid. In other words, they ensure that the government's net worth on a present value basis is positive.

The conditions in equations (7) or (8) and (9) have constituted the core of many empirical studies on fiscal sustainability.[22] In some studies, the focus lies on testing whether the primary deficit or the debt-to-GDP ratio, or the discounted debt-to-GDP ratio are stationary over a sufficiently long time period.[23] As discussed below, stationarity of these variables is necessary for solvency but not a sufficient condition for fiscal sustainability.[24] In other studies, some arbitrary steady-state, debt-to-GDP ratio is defined, which is then used to assess the sustainability of the current fiscal policy on the basis of the current level of debt and average growth rates of expenditure, revenue, interest rates, and GDP growth.

[21]Note that the transversality condition is irrelevant if the real interest rate is, on average, lower than the GDP growth rate. However, if this case were relevant, the economy could be dynamically inefficient (see Abel and others, 1989).

[22]See Hamilton and Flavin (1986), Wilcox (1989), and Buiter and Patel (1992), among others.

[23]The discounted public debt is defined by the continuous application of the transversality condition in equation (5), starting from the first data point in the sample. In Table 3.3 the discounted net public debt for Lebanon is shown. Since the transversality condition in equation (5) is only relevant if the real interest rate exceeds the growth rate, it is only reported for the period 1994–97.

[24]Note, however, that the debt-to-GDP ratio does not need to be stationary to satisfy the transversality condition, which only limits its growth rate.

In many circumstances, the concept of fiscal solvency is not terribly useful for policy analysis for the following reasons:

(1) While it seems reasonable and pragmatic to require that the debt-to-GDP ratio be a stationary time series in a very large data sample, the requirement is weak in that it is consistent with almost any positive mean value for this variable. Even a shift in the long-run debt-to-GDP value from, say, 40 percent to 100 percent, does not violate the solvency conditions. From a general macroeconomic perspective, however, such changes would not be minor, since their implications for growth and macroeconomic policies are likely to be substantial.

(2) In many countries, the time span covered by the data sample is insufficient to allow for a meaningful distinction between stationary and nonstationary time series for the primary deficit and the debt-to-GDP ratio.

(3) Macroeconomic variables, such as the real interest rate and growth, are usually taken as given in the derivation and testing of equations (3) and (4). However, fiscal policies, in particular if they are perceived to violate solvency conditions, have repercussions on financial market prices and growth. The solvency and sustainability of certain fiscal policies, therefore, can not be assessed without taking into account macroeconomic policies in general as well as the interaction between macroeconomic variables and policies. For example, if a government embarks on a fiscal program that, in the perception of financial markets, implies an explosive path for the government debt, financial market participants would require higher and higher interest rates to be compensated for the risks and would eventually refuse to acquire or hold government bonds. The government would then be forced to abandon its unsustainable program.

(4) Another problem of the interaction of fiscal policies and other macroeconomic variables is that the range of fiscal policies consistent with solvency can depend on the overall macroeconomic policy mix. For example, the exchange rate regime, which, through its implications for monetary policy, can narrow the set of fiscal sustainable policies, as often demonstrated by many episodes of debt-related currency crises in the case of fixed exchange rates.

For Lebanon, the problems associated with the notion of fiscal solvency are particularly relevant. It is obvious that increases of the debt-to-GDP ratio of 8 to 10 percentage points or more a year would result if the large primary deficits during 1991–97 were maintained for a long time and if the growth-adjusted real interest rate were positive. Over time, such a policy would be perceived to violate the conditions in equations (3) and (4) and would thus become unsustainable, as investors would refuse to purchase government bonds. However, since these large primary deficits are temporary during a reconstruction, the standard methods of assessing fiscal solvency are impractical. For Lebanon, the principal issue in the assessment of the sustainability of its fiscal policies is the degree of adjustment—defined as the reduction in the primary deficit—that is needed to ensure that a manageable debt-to-GDP ratio level can be maintained over the medium term.

References

Abel, Andrew, and others, 1989, "Assessing Dynamic Efficiency: Theory and Evidence," *Review of Economic Studies,* Vol. 56 (January), pp. 1–20.

Barro, Robert J., 1974, "Are Government Bonds Net Wealth," *Journal of Political Economy,* Vol. 82 (December), pp. 1095–1117.

_____, 1979, "On the Determination of the Public Debt," *Journal of Political Economy,* Vol. 87 (October), pp. 940–71.

_____, and Xavier Sala-i-Martin, 1992, "Public Finance in Models of Economic Growth," *Review of Economic Studies,* Vol. 59 (October), pp. 645–61.

_____, 1995, *Economic Growth* (New York: McGraw-Hill).

Bernheim, B. Douglas, 1987, "Ricardian Equivalence: An Evaluation of Theory and Evidence," NBER Working Paper 2330 (Cambridge, Massachusetts: National Bureau of Economic Research), pp. 263–303.

Blanchard, Olivier J., 1990, "Suggestions for a New Set of Fiscal Indicators," OECD Working Paper No. 79 (Paris: OECD).

_____, Jean-Claude Chouraqui, Robert P. Hagemann, and Nicola Sartor, 1990, "The Sustainability of Fiscal Policy: New Answers to an Old Question," *OECD Economic Studies,* No. 15 (Autumn), pp. 7–36.

Buiter, Willem, 1985, "A Guide to Public Sector Debt and Deficits," *Economic Policy,* Vol. 1 (November), pp. 13–79.

_____, 1997, "Aspects of Fiscal Performance in Some Transition Economies Under Fund-Supported Programs," IMF Working Paper 97/31 (Washington: International Monetary Fund).

_____, and Urjit R. Patel, 1992, "Debt, Deficits, and Inflation: An Application to the Public Finances of India," *Journal of Public Economics,* Vol. 47 (March), pp. 171–205.

Dornbusch, Rudiger, and Mario Draghi, eds., 1990, *Public Debt Management: Theory and History* (Cambridge; New York: Cambridge University Press).

Eken, Sena, Paul Cashin, S. Nuri Erbas, Jose Martelino, and Adnan Mazarei, 1995, *Economic Dislocation and Recovery in Lebanon,* IMF Occasional Paper No. 120 (Washington: International Monetary Fund).

Ford, Robert, and Douglas Laxton, 1995, "World Public Debt and Real Interest Rates," IMF Working Paper 95/30 (Washington: International Monetary Fund).

Hamilton, James D., and Marjorie A. Flavin, 1986, "On the Limitations of Government Borrowing: A Framework for Empirical Testing," *American Economic Review,* Vol. 76 (September), pp. 808–19.

Helbling, Thomas, and Robert Wescott, 1995, "The Global Real Interest Rate," *Staff Studies for the World Economic Outlook,* World Economic and Financial Surveys (Washington: International Monetary Fund), pp. 1–27.

Makdisi, Samir A., 1987, "Political Conflict and Economic Performance in Lebanon, 1975–1987," *Bulletin Trimestriel,* Banque du Liban (Second and Third Quarters), pp. 4–12.

Mongelli, Francesco P., 1996, "The Effects of the European Economic and Monetary Union (EMU) on National Fiscal Sustainability," IMF Working Paper 96/72 (Washington: International Monetary Fund).

Obstfeld, Maurice, 1994, "The Logic of Currency Crises," NBER Working Paper No. 4640 (Cambridge, Massachusetts: National Bureau of Economic Research).

Razin, Assaf, 1996, "Notes on Fiscal and External Sustainability" (unpublished; Washington: International Monetary Fund).

Saidi, Nasser, 1989, "Deficits, Inflation, and Depreciation: Lebanon's Experience, 1964–88," in *Politics and the Economy of Lebanon,* ed. by Nadim Shehadi and Bridget Harney (London: The Center for Lebanese Studies, Oxford University, and the School of Oriental and African Studies).

Tanzi, Vito, and Domenico Fanizza, 1995, "Fiscal Deficit and Public Debt in Industrial Countries, 1970–94," IMF Working Paper 95/49 (Washington: International Monetary Fund).

Tanzi, Vito, and Howell H. Zee, 1996, "Fiscal Policy and Long-Run Growth," IMF Working Paper 96/119 (Washington: International Monetary Fund).

Wilcox, David W., 1989, "The Sustainability of Government Deficits: Implications of the Present-Value Borrowing Constraint," *Journal of Money, Credit, and Banking,* Vol. 21 (August), pp. 291–306.

IV   Dynamics of Interest Rate Movements: An Empirical Study

Taline Urnéchlian with Sena Eken and Thomas Helbling

Interest rate differentials between short-term assets denominated in Lebanese pounds and comparable U.S. dollar assets have been large and positive since the 1980s. During that time, the large differentials reflected the war-related macroeconomic instability. However, they have continued to be large even after the end of 1992, when the authorities moved decisively to overcome the inflationary expectations, which had continued to prevail in the immediate postwar period, by adopting an exchange rate-based nominal anchor policy, which has been maintained since.

Positive interest rate differentials in the context of an exchange rate peg are a familiar phenomenon, reflecting inter alia the risks associated with future changes in the peg or in the exchange rate regime. They tend to be persistent. In the European Monetary System, for example, the convergence to German interest rates was gradual and occurred only together with a general convergence in macroeconomic policies. From this perspective, the persistent positive interest differential in Lebanon reflects its status as a postwar economy, overcoming a legacy of significant macroeconomic instability during the war. The phenomenon to explain is not the existence of an interest rate differential that is positive on average, but rather the speed with which it will decline, given the recent progress toward macroeconomic stability. The issue is of interest to the Lebanese authorities because the high Lebanese pound interest rates have led to a substantial burden on the budget and monetary policy.

Analytical Framework

The analytical framework of this section is based on a linear factor model designed to explain the systematic excess return on Lebanese pound treasury bills compared with U.S. dollar papers. The excess

returns reflect systematic deviations from the uncovered interest parity condition, a standard benchmark in international finance.

Uncovered Interest Parity

According to the uncovered interest parity hypothesis, the nominal return differential between two assets that are identical in all respects except for the currency of denomination is equal to the expected exchange rate change over the holding period in asset-market equilibrium. In a small open economy that faces a given level of world interest rates, capital mobility should ensure the equalization of expected net yields so that the domestic interest rate, less the expected rate of depreciation, would equal the world rate. More formally, let s_t be the logarithm of the spot exchange rate at time t, defined as the domestic currency price of one U.S. dollar; let $E(s_{t+n/t})$ be the expected value of the logarithm of the exchange rate n periods ahead, conditional on information available at time t, and let i_t and i_t^* be the period t nominal interest rates on domestic and foreign assets with n periods remaining to maturity, respectively. Then, the uncovered interest parity (UIP) hypothesis can be written as:

$$E(s_{t+n/t}) - s_t = i_t - i_t^*. \qquad (1)$$

It should be noted that $E(s_{t+n/t})$ is not an observable variable. To test equation (1) empirically, assumptions about the process through which financial market participants formulate expectations have to be made. Recent research has focused on the assumption of rational expectations. More specifically, the following two assumptions have to be made to obtain an empirical model with rational expectations. First, the realized spot exchange rate is equal to its expected value plus a forecast error with zero mean:

$$s_{t+n} = E(s_{t+n/t}) + \epsilon_{t+n}, E(\epsilon_{t+n/t}) = 0. \qquad (2)$$

Second, the foreign exchange market is weakly efficient, in the sense that market expectations of the

Note: The initial draft of this section was prepared by Taline Urnéchlian of the Banque du Liban while she was a summer intern in the IMF's Middle Eastern Department.

future spot rate are always conditional on an information set that includes past forecast errors of the exchange rate. This second assumption, taken in conjunction with the first, also implies that the stochastic process (ϵ_t) is a white noise process, that is, the forecast errors are mutually uncorrelated at all lags:

$$E(\epsilon_t, \epsilon_{t+j}) = 0, {}_{j \neq t}. \tag{3}$$

Over the last two decades, numerous authors using a variety of data, sources, and estimation techniques have decisively rejected the uncovered interest rate parity condition, under the rational expectations hypothesis (e.g., Cumby and Obstfeld (1980, 1984) or Lewis (1994)). In particular, it has been shown that the forecast errors ϵ_{t+n} are serially correlated and, sometimes, not even stationary, thereby violating one of the basic principles of the rational expectations hypothesis.

Excess Returns

In view of the empirical evidence, ϵ_{t+n} should not be assumed to be a white noise forecast error. More appropriately, it should be considered to represent a systematic excess return, which is defined as:

$$\epsilon_{t+n} = s_t - s_{t+n} + i_t - i_t^* \tag{4}$$

The most compelling explanation for a systematic excess return is the presence of a risk premium between assets denominated in different currencies. To provide content to this argument requires a theory of the determinants of risk. Despite the theoretical advances in modeling risk (e.g., Cox, and Ingersoll, 1985), the determinants of risk are still not well understood, and recent empirical research has not yet offered consistent results.[1]

The excess return compensates investors for the risk in cross-border asset holdings. Two specific not necessarily uncorrelated risk factors can be distinguished. First, the country risk factor encompasses factors such as political risks that can hamper the cross-border transfers of both returns and principals. Second, the macroeconomic risk includes factors that cause future exchange rate changes. The nature of the macroeconomic risk premium depends on the exchange rate regime. Under a floating exchange rate regime, exchange rate changes occur frequently and tend to have a time-varying distribution; it is not surprising that many authors have found a time-varying distribution for excess returns defined ac-

cording to equation (4).[2] Under any regime of pegged exchange rates, the issue of the expected exchange rate changes becomes more delicate, because the peg might either be abolished or be changed in the future. This possibility raises the issue of the "peso problem."[3]

The peso problem reflects expectations of regime changes in an unstable environment. In many circumstances, countries pursue macroeconomic policies that are inconsistent with the exchange rate peg in the long run. Investors, therefore, expect the peg to be abandoned or changed in the future, but might be uncertain about the timing of these events. They base their expectations on a subjective probability distribution that differs from the empirical distribution that can be deduced from past realizations. Strictly speaking, the term "peso problem" is typically used when a regime change has not yet been observed. It is therefore impossible to detect the probability distribution underlying investors' expectations.[4]

The "peso problem" has two implications. First, the uncovered interest parity hypothesis is rejected even if the two assets under consideration are perfect substitutes otherwise. Second, a tricky identification problem arises. As long as there is a probability of a regime change or an exchange rate devaluation, and without sufficient observed realizations of such events, it is impossible to distinguish empirically between rational expectations influenced by a peso problem and irrational expectations. Rogoff (1980) pointed out that when the market expects a discrete change in policy, exchange rate expectations will induce serially correlated forecast errors, with a mean that can be different from zero.[5]

Recent research has gone one step further by identifying the factors that affect this excess return or the probability of a regime change, or both. Many au-

---

[1]See, among many others, Cochrane and Hansen (1992), Lewis (1994), and Kocherlakota (1996).

[2]See, for example, Engel and Rodrigues (1989) or Mayfield and Murphy (1992).

[3]The first use of the term "peso problem" is attributed to Milton Friedman in his examination of the Mexican peso market during the early 1970s, where deposit rates remained substantially above U.S. dollar interest rates, even though the exchange rate was fixed. Friedman argued that this interest differential reflected the market's expectations of a devaluation of the peso. Subsequently, in 1976, the peso was devalued by 46 percent and was allowed to float thereafter.

[4]In empirical studies, however, the problem often remains relevant because only a few regime changes are typically observed during a given time period, so that standard distributions used in empirical research provide bad approximations.

[5]Recent empirical work showed that peso problems can have significant effects on the forecast errors. For example, Lewis (1990) found that the presence of a peso problem during the period of interest rates targeting in the United States induced sizable effects upon excess returns on longer-term bonds and allowed interest rates to fluctuate widely.

thors have linked the time-varying risk premium to macroeconomic fundamentals and indicator variables.[6] In some studies, linear factor models are used to explain excess returns:

$$\in_{t+n} = a + \sum \beta^i X_t^i + u_{t+n} \qquad (5)$$

where the vector of explanatory variables X_t^i represents fundamentals and indicators available at time t, and where u_{t+n} is a stationary process with zero mean.[7] These variables are different for each country, and depend on the country-specific economic structure. Therefore, they will be determined later in the discussion, after reviewing some of Lebanon's economic features.

Macroeconomic and Financial Developments, 1985–97

During the last part of the civil war (1985–89), a significant degree of macroeconomic (and political) instability prevailed.[8] Large budget deficits were monetized, and inflation was accelerating. Moreover, the destruction and loss of capital, both human and physical, were particularly severe during the period, and real GDP declined. All these developments were reflected in a rapid decline of the external value of the Lebanese pound against the major currencies, a sharp increase in dollarization, and capital outflows (Figure 4.1).

One year after the conclusion of the Taef agreement at the end of 1989, a government of national unity was reinstated, and a period of economic normalization and recovery started. Progress was nevertheless slow, and political uncertainty and macroeconomic fragility remained significant. Inflation rates remained high, and the Lebanese pound depreciated further, particularly in the first three quarters of 1992. It was only in October 1992, after the appointment of Prime Minister Hariri, that reconstruction and stabilization began.

An exchange-rate-based nominal anchor policy—targeting a slight nominal appreciation of the Lebanese pound against the U.S. dollar—has been at the core of the government's stabilization efforts. The policy has been successful in stabilizing expec-

Figure 4.1. Lebanese Pound–U.S. Dollar Exchange Rate and Interest Differential

Lebanese Pounds per U.S. Dollar

Interest Differential in Percentage Points on the Basis of Three-Month Treasury Bills

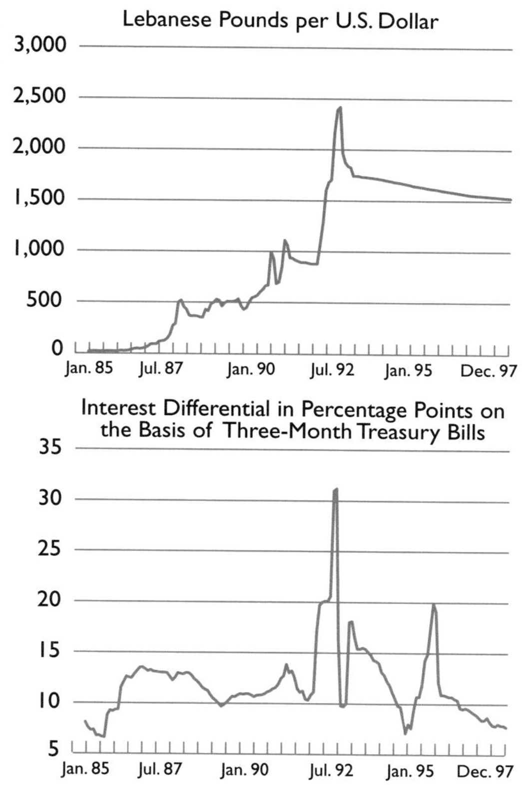

Sources: Data provided by the Lebanese authorities; and IMF, *International Financial Statistics.*

---

[6]See Caramazza (1993), Chen and Giovannini (1993), and Holden and Vickøren (1996) for recent studies.

[7]By specifying equation (5), it is assumed that the excess returns $\in_t$ as well as the explanatory variables X_t^i are stationary, that is, integrated of order zero $I(0)$. If, however, the excess returns $\in_t$ were $I(1)$, then the factor model would have to be formulated as an error correction model (Engle and Granger (1987)).

[8]See Eken and others (1995) for a more detailed description of macroeconomic developments during the war years.

tations, and inflation rates have been rapidly reduced to single-digit levels. The overall macroeconomic situation, however, remains difficult with large budget deficits, associated growing public debt, large current account deficit, and occasional episodes of domestic and regional political uncertainties. Under the circumstances, and given the virtual absence of restrictions on capital account transactions, monetary policy has born a heavy burden, as high and flexible interest rates have been necessary to ensure the exchange rate peg and to allow for a comfortable cushion of foreign exchange reserves. The high interest rates are reflected both in the excess return differential and the UIP Lebanese pound–U.S. dollar exchange rate—the exchange rate that would prevail if the uncovered interest parity between Lebanese pound and U.S. dollar assets applied. For the period December 1992 to December 1996, the UIP exchange rate has constantly been more depreciated than the actual exchange rate, confirming the bias in its capacity as a predictor of future exchange rate changes found elsewhere (Figure 4.2).

To ensure the exchange rate peg, monetary policy and public debt management have been closely coordinated (see Section V). The authorities have set monetary policy parameters, particularly the interest rates in the primary sales of treasury bills, such that official foreign exchange reserves cover a significant share of the domestic currency debt, which is largely short-term and therefore constitutes a potential quasi-monetary liability. In times of favorable financial market sentiments, treasury bills above and beyond the financing needs of the treasury's budget

needs have been issued—to sterilize foreign exchange inflows through matching increases in the accounts of the treasury with the central bank. This cushion has allowed the authorities some temporary interest rate smoothing during times of financial market turbulence. In this sense, both treasury bill interest rates and official foreign exchange reserves are not only reflecting the preferences and expectations of investors, but also the monetary policy reaction function of the authorities. The negative relationship between changes in the interest differential on Lebanese pound and U.S. dollar treasury bills and changes in the ratio of gross official foreign exchange reserves to treasury bills shown in Figure 4.3

Figure 4.2. Uncovered Interest Parity and Excess Returns

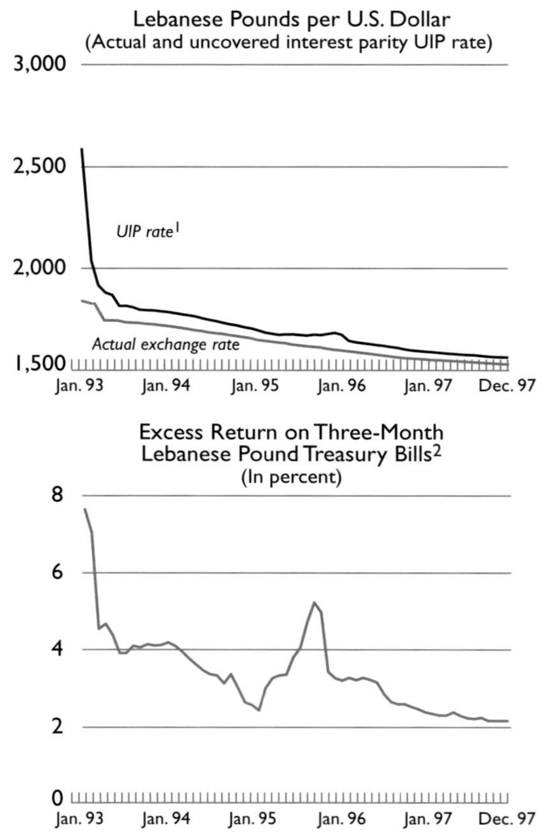

Lebanese Pounds per U.S. Dollar
(Actual and uncovered interest parity UIP rate)

Excess Return on Three-Month
Lebanese Pound Treasury Bills[2]
(In percent)

Sources: Data provided by the Lebanese authorities; and IMF, *International Financial Statistics.*
[1]Exchange rate given by the requirement that the lagged three-month interest rate differential is equal to the actual three-month exchange rate change.
[2]On a quarterly basis in comparison with three-month U.S. dollar treasury bills.

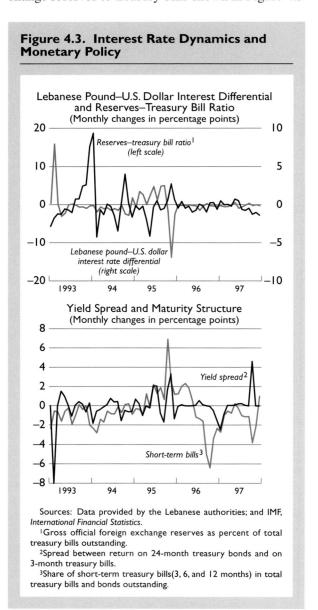

Figure 4.3. Interest Rate Dynamics and Monetary Policy

Lebanese Pound–U.S. Dollar Interest Differential and Reserves–Treasury Bill Ratio
(Monthly changes in percentage points)

Yield Spread and Maturity Structure
(Monthly changes in percentage points)

Sources: Data provided by the Lebanese authorities; and IMF, *International Financial Statistics.*
[1]Gross official foreign exchange reserves as percent of total treasury bills outstanding.
[2]Spread between return on 24-month treasury bonds and on 3-month treasury bills.
[3]Share of short-term treasury bills(3, 6, and 12 months) in total treasury bills and bonds outstanding.

could be a reflection of the monetary authorities' policy to ensure a sufficient coverage of short-term Lebanese pound debt by reserves. Moreover, the positive correlation between the change in the yield spread (between 24-month treasury bonds and 3-month treasury bills) and changes in the share of short-term treasury bills in the total treasury bills and bonds outstanding provides evidence of the authorities' attempt to offset the impact of market pressures on the maturity structure of the domestic currency debt.

An Empirical Examination of the Interest Rate Differential Between the Lebanese Pound and the U.S. Dollar

In this subsection, the interest rate dynamics in Lebanon during the period 1993–96 is examined empirically from three different angles. First, the basic time series statistics for the deviations from the uncovered interest parity condition are analyzed to determine whether they have been significant. Second, the interaction between monetary policy and the interest dynamics is investigated. Finally, an empirical model that relates the excess return to macroeconomic fundamentals is estimated.

Testing for the Uncovered Interest Rate Parity

The tests of the uncovered interest rate parity hypothesis are based on the analysis of the time series properties of the quarterly excess return $\in_{t+3}$ on three-month Lebanese pound treasury bills relative to three-month U.S. dollar treasury bills.[9] The analysis was conducted using monthly data, with the sample covering the period 1993–97. The sample was chosen because it encompasses a period during which the authorities were implementing an exchange-rate-based nominal anchor policy, and during which treasury bills sold in auctions were the most important Lebanese pound assets.

The basic statistics presented in Table 4.1 indicate that, during the period 1993–97, the mean excess return was equal 13.9 percent (on an annual basis) and was significantly different from zero, and that the interest rate differential between three-month Lebanese pound and U.S. dollar treasury bills systematically overstated the change in the Lebanese pound–U.S. dollar exchange rate over the subsequent three months. Moreover, the excess return series displays serial correlation, which indicates that the risk premium and exchange rate expectations reflected in this variable were changing only gradually

Table 4.1. Analysis of Excess Returns[1]

	$\in_t$	$\Delta\in_t$
Sample	1993M1–97M12	1993M1–96M12
Mean	0.033	–0.0009
Standard deviation	0.009	0.004
RHO(1)[2]		
QP(12)[3]	0.746	0.209
	122.99	5.036
	[0.000]	[0.984]
PPF(2)[4]	–4.437	–5.475
ADF(1)[5]	–4.526	–5.316
Normality[6]	11.308	98.952
	[0.043]	[0.000]

Source: IMF staff calculations based on data provided by the authorities.
[1]Marginal significance levels in brackets.
[2]First-order autocorrelation coefficient.
[3]Portmanteau test statistics, follow χ^2-distribution.
[4]Philips-Perron unit root test, 2 lags.
[5]Augmented Dickey-Fuller unit root test, 2 lags.
[6]Test statistics follows χ^2-distribution.

over time. The hypothesis is supported by the sample mean of the first difference of the excess return (significantly different from zero at a 5.3 percent level), which suggests that the excess return was declining by 0.4 percent a year during 1993–97.

Monetary Policy, Lebanese Pound–U.S. Dollar Interest Rate Differential, and Yield Spread

As argued earlier, the interest rate differential between three-month Lebanese pound and U.S. dollar treasury bills and the yield spread between 24-month Lebanese pound treasury bonds and three-month treasury bills may not only reflect the expectations and preferences of investors, but also the reaction function of the monetary authorities. To study the interaction between monetary policy and the interest differential and the yield spread, respectively, two bivariate vector autoregressive models (VARs) were estimated. The results will be helpful for the subsequent specification of an empirical model for the excess returns $\in_{t+3}$ because they determine whether the role of monetary policy in the determination of this variable needs to be taken into account in the empirical analysis.

The first bivariate VAR involves the changes in the interest differential on three-month Lebanese pound and U.S. dollar treasury bills, $i_t - I_t^*$,[10] and

---

[9]Quarterly excess returns are calculated according to equation (4).

[10]The interest rate differential on these three-month treasury bills is referred to as interest differential in the remainder of the paper.

changes in the ratio of gross foreign exchange reserves R_t to treasury bills T_t. If the monetary authorities target a range for the ratio of reserves to treasury bills by using the interest differential as an instrument, then past realizations of the instrument have some predictive power for the current value of the target variable while past realizations of the target should not have any predictive power for the current value of the instrument. The Granger causality tests reported in Table 4.2 do not confirm the hypothesis that there has been a target-instrument relationship between the ratio of gross foreign exchange reserves to treasury bills and the interest rate differential during the period 1993–97. For the period 1993–96, however, such a target-instrument relationship could

be found. It is noteworthy that a VAR analysis for the period 1993–96 involving the levels of the interest differential and the ratio of reserves to treasury bills does not indicate any clear-cut directions of Granger causality. These results suggest that the monetary authorities tried to avoid sharp changes in the ratio of foreign exchange reserves to treasury bills during 1993–96 rather than targeting a specific value for the variable.

The second bivariate VAR involves the changes in the secondary market yield spread between Lebanese pound 24-month treasury bonds and 3-month treasury bills, $i_t^{24}-i_t$,[11] and changes in the share of short-term treasury bills ST_t (up to 12 months) in total treasury bills and bonds T_t outstanding. If the monetary authorities target a range for the share of short-term treasury bills in total treasury bills using the yield spread as an instrument, then past realizations of the instrument should again have some predictive power for the current value of the target variable. The Granger causality tests reported in Table 4.2 do not confirm the hypothesis that there has been a target-instrument relationship between the share of short-term treasury bills in total treasury bills and bonds outstanding during the period 1993–97.[12] In fact, the direction of causality is the reverse. Changes in ratio of short-term to total treasury bills precede changes in the yield spread. One reason for this result could be that the monetary authorities react to changes in investors' preferences regarding the maturity structure with a lag. In particular, it could be that changes in the maturity structure of the flows rather than the composition of the stock are targeted. These results suggest that changes in the maturity structure were not of the same immediate importance to the monetary authorities as changes in the ratio of gross official foreign exchange reserves to treasury bills.

A Linear Factor Model Explaining Excess Returns

Explaining the excess return ϵ_{t+3} with a linear factor model aims at relating the risk premium captured in this variable to macroeconomic fundamentals and to political factors, which are captured by a dummy variable. As shown above, the recent empirical evidence does not suggest that monetary policy actions had a strong direct impact on the dependent variable. In the empirical analysis, the following explanatory variables were included: the growth rate of

Table 4.2. Monetary Policy, the Lebanese Pound–U.S. Dollar Interest Differential, and Yield Spread: Granger Causality Tests[1]

A. VAR 1: Lebanese Pound–U.S. Dollar Interest Differential and the Ratio of Reserves to Treasury Bills[2] 1993M1–97M12		
	$\Delta(i_{t-1} - I^*_{t-1})$	$\Delta(R_{t-1}/T_{t-1})$
$\Delta(i_t - I^*_t)$	1.58 (0.21)	3.12 (0.08)
$\Delta(R_t/T_t)$	0.00 (0.99)	8.08 (0.01)
1993M1–96M12		
	$\Delta(i_{t-1} - I^*_{t-1})$	$\Delta(R_{t-1}/T_{t-1})$
$\Delta(i_t - I^*_t)$	5.67 (0.02)	0.09 (0.76)
$\Delta(R_t/T_t)$	48.50 (0.00)	0.92 (0.34)
B. VAR II: Yield Spread and the Ratio of Short-Term to Total Treasury Bills[3] 1993M1–97M12		
	$\Delta(i^{24}_{t-1} - i_{t-1})$	$\Delta(ST_{t-1}/T_{t-1})$
$\Delta(it^{24} - i_t)$	2.13 (0.13)	2.45 (0.10)
$\Delta(ST_t/T_t)$	0.72 (0.49)	22.34 (0.00)

Source: IMF staff calculations based on data provided by the authorities.

[1]F-test of the null hypothesis that the explanatory variables in the columns can be excluded from the equation with the variable in the row as dependent variable (marginal significance level in parentheses). For example, the F-test statistic of the null hypothesis that lagged values of the ratio of reserves to treasury bills have no impact on the current period interest differential is 0.09.

[2]Based on first-order VARs.

[3]Based on a second-order VAR.

---

[11]The yield spread between Lebanese pound 24-month treasury bonds and three-month treasury bills is referred to as yield spread in the remainder of the paper.

[12]Estimating the same VAR for the period 1993–96 yields similar results.

the domestic public debt, the growth rate of M2, the growth rate of domestic credit, the growth rate of the real exchange rate, the first lag of the dependent variable, and a dummy variable. With the exception of the last two variables, all were lagged by one period to avoid simultaneity problems.

The model is based on the following rationale:

- Expectations about future events, particularly regime changes that are unrelated to current macroeconomic fundamentals, are captured by the first lag of the endogenous variable. As shown by the literature on peso problems, expectations about future regime changes tend to be persistent, suggesting a positive relationship between the current excess return and its lagged value.
- The variation of the gross foreign reserves of the central bank is a measure for the exchange rate risk in Lebanon perceived by investors. Since the central bank is pursuing an exchange-rate-based nominal anchor policy, changes in the perceived exchange risk and therefore demand for Lebanese pound assets would be reflected as a variation in gross reserves. However, there is also feedback from the level of gross foreign exchange reserves to the perceived exchange rate risk. Accordingly, an increase in the growth of foreign exchange reserves would ceteris paribus lower the risk of an exchange rate regime change and then lower the excess return.
- The fiscal deficit, which can be approximated by the percentage variation of the domestic debt, is a good indicator for the country's creditworthiness. This variable can be expected to be positively correlated with interest rates because investors require larger returns to increase the share of treasury bills in their portfolio.[13]
- Similarly, the ratio of M2 to M3 is an indicator for investors' expectations, because it reflects the demand for Lebanese pound assets by residents.[14] An increase in this ratio would, ceteris paribus, lead to a decrease in the excess return.

- The growth rate of domestic credit to the private sector is used as an indicator for real sector growth. Given the lack of sufficiently long time series for summary measures of real sector activity, the domestic credit variable serves as a proxy variable. An increase in private sector credit growth, being interpreted as an increase in GDP growth, would, ceteris paribus, reduce the fiscal deficit as a percent of GDP and reduce the supply of domestic assets, but increase the demand for domestic assets, thereby reducing the excess return.
- The real effective exchange rate is an indicator for the external sector viability. An increase in the growth rate of this variable would reduce the competitiveness of the economy and, ceteris paribus, reduce the external current account balance and increase the need for capital inflows. This would require an increase in the excess return.
- The 0–1 dummy variable takes the value 1 during periods of heightened political uncertainty. These periods are related to the uncertainty about the presidential elections in 1995, the cabinet crisis following Prime Minister Hariri's resignation threat in early 1995, and the bombings in April 1996. The impact of political uncertainty on the excess return can be expected to be positive.

The estimation results, which are presented in the appendix, imply that current macroeconomic fundamentals explain only a small fraction of the movement in the excess return on treasury bills during the period of January 1993–December 1997. Only the ratio of M2 to M3 turned out to be significant, with the expected negative sign. All other variables, except for the first lag of the dependent variable and the dummy variable, were insignificant. These results suggest that the demand for Lebanese pound assets by resident investors is important in determining the excess return and that expectations about future exchange rate changes are not tightly linked to other current macroeconomic fundamentals. This is consistent with a hypothesis that is often stated in Lebanon, namely, that expectation-linked, sociopolitical conditions are the dominant determinants of local financial market conditions.

These results may also reflect other factors. The sample period is short, covering a period of recovery, reconstruction, and stabilization, during which the excess return has, on average, been declining. Current and past realizations of macroeconomic fundamentals might therefore contain little information for future macroeconomic developments since their behavioral pattern is changing during such a period of transition. Signaling future policy actions could be much more important under these circumstances.

---

[13]In principle, the growth rate of the domestic public debt in excess of the growth rate of wealth should be used. However, due to data limitations and difficulties in defining the relevant wealth variables with capital mobility, the simple model growth rate of domestic debt is used.

[14]M2 is the sum of currency in circulation and of Lebanese pouund sight and demand deposits. Given the very limited Lebanese pound lending to the private sector, bank holdings of treasury bills are the major counterpart of M2 in the balance sheet of the monetary sector. It should be noted, however, that the domestic public debt is also held directly by the nonbank public, including nonresident investors. The latter are not allowed to hold Lebanese pound deposits with the banking system. The indicator properties of M2 are therefore different from those of the growth rate of the domestic public debt, since the latter variable captures changes in the asset holding by both resident and nonresident investors.

Furthermore, lagged values of the growth rates of domestic public debt and the foreign exchange reserves are likely to have weak leading indicator properties with respect to the excess return as a result of the conduct of monetary policy discussed above.

Conclusions

Domestic interest rates in Lebanon have exceeded world market rates by a large margin in the context of an exchange-rate-based nominal anchor policy that targeted a slight nominal appreciation of the Lebanese pound against the U.S. dollar. The average interest rate differential between three-month treasury bills denominated in Lebanese pounds and U.S. dollars has amounted to about 12 percent during 1993–96, implying an average annualized excess return of about 16 percent.

The main conclusions from the empirical analysis of this interest differential may be summarized as follows:

- The uncovered interest rate parity relationship does not hold in Lebanon. As a result, interest rate differentials between the Lebanese pound and the U.S. dollar denominated similar assets are not good predictors for the future exchange rate.
- Deviations from uncovered interest rate parity suggest the existence of a risk premium, possibly related to a peso problem.
- A model that incorporates macroeconomic fundamentals, such as changes in money supply, helps explain the excess return on domestic assets, albeit to a limited degree only. The empirical model also provides evidence that shocks and expectations about future events that are not captured by current fundamentals have a long-lasting effect on excess returns, which indicates that credibility and reputation effects are important.

These findings suggest that interest rates are responsive to policy developments as well as to external shocks in Lebanon. Therefore, the authorities should reduce the vulnerability of the economy to exogenous shocks and implement policies that enhance credibility and reduce the risk premium in interest rates. With regard to the latter, a front-loaded fiscal adjustment and a sustainable macroeconomic policy mix are crucial.

Appendix. Explaining Excess Returns in Lebanon, 1993–97

This appendix, based on the linear factor model discussed at the beginning of the section, tries to set up an empirical model that relates the excess return ϵ_{t+3} to macroeconomic fundamentals, to its own lagged value, and to a dummy variable, denoted with I_t, that captures periods of heightened political uncertainty.

The set of currently observed macroeconomic fundamentals includes the growth rate of gross official foreign exchange reserves (converted into Lebanese pounds), denoted with R, the growth rate of the domestic public debt, D, the ratio of $M2$ to $M3$, the growth rate of domestic credit, DC, and the percentage change of the real exchange rate, RER.

All explanatory variables except for the dummy variable (and the lagged value of the dependent variable) are lagged by one period to avoid problems related to the simultaneity between the dependent and the current period explanatory variables. These problems arise because the excess return during the period 1993–97 is largely determined by the interest differential given the steady and predictable Lebanese pound appreciation. The lagged explanatory variables therefore have the character of leading indicator variables. Moreover, the model is also specified using natural logarithms for the excess return and other variables in levels to reduce the volatility of the estimation error.[15]

The empirical model for the excess return can therefore be written as:

$$\ln(\epsilon_{t+3}) = \alpha + \beta_1\ln(\epsilon_{t+2}) + \beta_2\Delta\ln R_{t-1}$$
$$+ \beta_3\Delta\ln D_{t-1} + \beta_4\ln\frac{M2_{t-1}}{M3_{t-1}}$$
$$+ \beta_5\Delta\ln DC_{t-1} + \beta_6\Delta\ln RER_{t-1} + \beta_7 I_t + \eta_t, \quad (6)$$

where η_t denotes a residual.

Equation (5) was estimated with ordinary least squares for the period January 1993 to December 1997.[16] The results, which are reported in Table 4.3, show that many variables were insignificant, including the growth rate of gross official foreign exchange reserves, the growth rate of the domestic public debt, the growth rate of domestic credit, and the growth rate of the real exchange rate.

The final empirical model that was estimated after using Wald tests to reduce the number of explanatory variables is reported in the last column of Table

[15]The estimation of the model in levels yields results, that are qualitatively similar to those reported. The residuals, however, have the natural characteristics of a time series process with autoregressive condition heteroskedasticity (ARCH). Estimating an ARCH model would not provide any additional insight, however, and the log specification allows one to avoid the problem.

[16]In a first stage, unit root tests were applied to all the explanatory variables for the period January 1993–December 1996. All of them turned out to be stationary.

Table 4.3. Explaining Excess Returns, 1993M1–1997M12[1]

Dependent variable	$\ln(\epsilon_{t+3})$	$\ln(\epsilon_{t+3})$
Estimation method	OLS	OLS
Explanatory variables		
$\ln(\epsilon_{t+2})$	0.658 (0.126)	0.700 (0.082)
$\Delta\ln R_{t-1}$	0.602 (0.645)	
$\Delta\ln D_{t-1}$	−0.257 (0.358)	
$\Delta\ln DC_{t-1}$	−0.101 6.354	
$\Delta\ln RER_{t-1}$	−0.936 (0.921)	
$\Delta\ln (M2_{t-1}/M3_{t-1})$	−0.565 (0.209)	−0.435 (0.113)
I_t	0.057 (0.029)	0.060 (0.025)
R^2	0.902	0.904
σ	0.083	0.082
D.W.	1.742	1.761
$AR(1-2)^2$	0.904 [0.411]	0.683 [0.509]
$ARCH(1)^3$	0.725 [0.399]	0.417 [0.521]
DF^4	−6.864	−6.913

Source: IMF staff calculations based on data provided by the authorities.

[1]Autocorrelation-heteroskedasticity constant standard errors in parentheses. Marginal significance levels in square brackets.

[2]Lagrange multiplier test for second-order autocorrelation in the residuals; the test statistics follows an *F*-distribution.

[3]Test statistics follows an *F*-distribution.

[4]Dickey-Fuller unit root tests applied to residuals (no constant included); test statistics denotes *t*-statistics.

4.3. Three variables turned out to be significant: the ratio of *M*2 to *M*3, the dummy variable, and the lagged value of the dependent variable.

Equation (5) was also estimated for different sample periods. Overall, the results are qualitatively similar, although the quantitative impact of the various explanatory variables on the excess return depends on the sample period.

References

Blejer, Mario I., 1982, "Interest Rate Differentials and Exchange Risk: Recent Argentine Experience," *Staff Papers*, International Monetary Fund, Vol. 29 (June), pp. 270–79.

Boughton, James M., 1987, "Test of the Performance of Reduced-Form Exchange Rate Models," *Journal of International Economics*, Vol. 23 (August), pp. 41–56.

Caramazza, Francesco, 1993, "French-German Interest Rate Differentials and Time-Varying Realignment Risk," *Staff Papers*, International Monetary Fund, Vol. 40 (September), pp. 567–83.

Chen, Zhaohui, and Alberto Giovannini, 1993, "The Determinants of Realignment Expectations Under the EMS: Some Empirical Regularities," NBER Working Paper, No. 4291 (Cambridge, Massachusetts: National Bureau of Economic Research).

Cochrane, John H., and Lars Peter Hansen, 1992, "Asset Pricing Explorations for Macroeconomics," *NBER Macroeconomics Annual*, pp. 115–82.

Cox, John C., and Jonathan E. Ingersoll Jr., 1985, "An Intertemporal General Equilibrium Model of Asset Prices," Econometrica, Vol. 53 (March), pp. 363–84.

Cumby, Robert E., 1988, "Is It Risk? Explaining Deviations from Uncovered Interest Parity," *Journal of Monetary Economics*, Vol. 22 (September), pp. 279–99.

———, and Maurice Obstfeld, 1982, "International Interest- Rates and Price-Level Linkages Under Flexible Exchange Rates: A Review of Recent Evidence," NBER Working Paper, No. 921 (Cambridge, Massachusetts: National Bureau of Economic Research).

———, 1980, "Exchange-Rate Expectations and Nominal Interest Differentials: A Test of Fisher Hypothesis," NBER Working Paper, No. 537 (Cambridge, Massachusetts: National Bureau of Economic Research).

Das Gupta, Dipak, and Bejoy Das Gupta, 1994, "Interest Rates in Open Economies: Real Interest Rate Parity, Exchange Rates and Country Risk in Industrial and Developing Countries," The World Bank, Policy Research Working Papers 1283 (Washington, World Bank)

Edwards, Sebastian, and Mohsin S. Khan, 1985, "Interest Rate Determination in Developing Countries," *Staff Papers*, International Monetary Fund, Vol. 32 (September), pp. 377–403.

Eken, Sena, Paul Cashin, S. Nuri Erbas, Jose Martelino, and Adnan Mazarei, 1995, *Economic Dislocation and Recovery in Lebanon*, IMF Occasional Paper No. 120 (Washington: International Monetary Fund).

Engel, Charles, and Anthony P. Rodrigues, 1989, "Tests of International CAPM with Time-Varying Covariances," *Journal of Applied Econometrics,* Vol. 4 (April), pp. 119–38.

Engle, Robert F., and Clive W.J. Granger, 1987, "Co-Integration and Error Correction: Representation, Estimation, and Testing," *Econometrica*, Vol. 55 (March), pp. 251–76.Hamilton, James D., 1994, *Time Series Analysis* (Princeton, New Jersey: Princeton University Press).

Holden, Steinar, 1996, "The Credibility of a Fixed Exchange Rate. How Reputation Is Gained or Lost," *Scandinavian Journal of Economics*, Vol. 98 (December), pp. 485–502.

Khor, Hoe E., and Liliana Rojas-Suarez, 1991, "Interest Rates in Mexico: The Role of Exchange Rate Expectations and International Creditworthiness," *Staff Papers*, International Monetary Fund, Vol. 38 (December), pp. 850–71.

Kocherlakota, Narayana R., 1996, "The Equity Premium: It's Still a Puzzle," *Journal of Economic Literature*, Vol. 24 (March), pp. 42–71.

Krasker, William S., 1980, "The 'Peso Problem' in Testing the Efficiency of Forward Exchange Markets," *Journal of Monetary Economics*, Vol. 6 (April), pp. 269–76.

Lewis, Karen K., 1990, "Was There a 'Peso Problem' in the U.S. Term Structure of Interest Rates: 1979–1982," NBER Working Paper No. 3282 (Cambridge, Massachusetts: National Bureau of Economic Research).

———, 1994, "International Financial Markets," in *Handbook of International Economics*, ed. by G. Grossman and K. Rogoff (Amsterdam: North Holland).

Mayfield, E. Scott, and Robert G. Murphy, 1992, "Interest Rate Parity and the Exchange Risk Premium: Evidence from Panel Data," *Economics Letters*, Vol. 40 (November), pp. 319–24.

Phillips, Peter C. B., Pierre Perron, 1987, "Testing for a Unit Root in Time Series Regression," *Biometrica*, Vol. 75, pp. 335–46.

Rogoff, Kenneth S., 1980, "Essays on Expectations and Exchange Rate Volatility" (unpublished Ph.D. dissertation; Cambridge, Massachusetts: Massachusetts Institute of Technology).

Schwert, William G., 1987, "Effects of Model Specification on Tests for Unit Roots in Macroeconomic Data," *Journal of Monetary Economics*, Vol. 20 (July), pp. 73–103 .

V   Issues in Public Debt Management

Thomas Helbling

Lebanon has a high and rapidly growing public debt. The government recognizes the risks associated with the recent public debt dynamics and plans to eliminate the primary budget deficit over the next two to three years. Nevertheless, the debt is likely to remain large in the medium term even with significant fiscal adjustment. Meanwhile, interest payments, which represented about 35 percent of government expenditure and absorbed 90 percent of budgetary revenue in 1997, will also remain large.

Many episodes in economic history have illustrated the problems that are associated with high levels of public debt. These problems include the dramatic impact of interest rate changes on borrowing costs and the perceived incentives to reduce the real value of both interest payments and the principal through surprise inflation. As a result, large stocks of outstanding public debt often lead to credibility problems, and macroeconomic conditions and policies become vulnerable to changes in financial market sentiments. The recent trend toward capital account and financial liberalization has only increased the probability of such debt-related difficulties and problems occurring.

Policy choices related to the structure of public debt fall in the domain of public debt management, an area to which an increasing number of countries have started to pay more attention.[1] Since Tobin's (1963) seminal paper on public debt management, discussion of debt-management strategies has often focused on the optimal maturity profile of public debt under the goals of minimizing interest costs and supporting the authorities' macroeconomic policies, particularly monetary policy. The maturity profile, however, is not the only dimension of an optimal debt structure, and recent research has focused on instruments such as foreign currency bonds and bonds indexed to the price level. With recent financial in-novations, the spectrum of instruments has expanded even further.

This section focuses on the policy problems associated with the current structure of Lebanon's public debt, which has been characterized by a large share of short-term treasury bills denominated in Lebanese pounds that have been issued at a high discount. It examines the scope for improving the structure of the debt such that both the risks and costs of the sizable debt stock are reduced. Such an improvement would both contribute to the authorities' fiscal adjustment efforts and lower the constraints on monetary policy. Nevertheless, it is important to recognize the limitations of public debt management, which remains a policy task subordinate to monetary and fiscal policy. In a medium-term perspective, it is primarily the level of public debt that matters for interest rates and for its implications for macroeconomic policies, while the effects of the structure of public debt tend to be secondary.

Lebanon's Public Debt and Its Management, 1991–97

Lebanon's sizable fiscal imbalances have been largely financed through the issue of short-term bonds denominated in Lebanese pounds. Refinancing this growing short-term public debt has been challenging given Lebanon's exchange-rate-based nominal anchor policy, a large external current account deficit, and the significant risks associated with domestic and regional political uncertainties. The close coordination between monetary policy and the management of public debt has been a key element for the success in maintaining nominal stability.

Level and Structure of Public Debt

During 1991–97, Lebanon's government finances resulted in primary deficits, reflecting large current expenditure (excluding interest payments), a slow recovery of the revenue-generation capacity, and the reconstruction-related surge in capital exenditure.

---

[1]In the United Kingdom, the treasury, in collaboration with the Bank of England, undertook a systematic review of public debt management in 1994/95 (see U.K. Treasury (1995)). Similarly, in Sweden, a Public Debt Management Commission recently reviewed Sweden's public debt management policies (See Swedish Ministry of Finance (1997)).

Accordingly, gross public debt rose from LL 2,737 billion at the end of 1991 to LL 23,504 billion at the end of 1997, which is equivalent to an increase from 66 percent of GDP to 102.7 percent. During the same period, net public debt, which does not include treasury bills issued for sterilization purposes increased from 58 percent of GDP to 97 percent. Within this period, two phases in the evolution of Lebanon's public debt can be distinguished (Figure 5.1). During 1991–93, both the gross and the net public debt as a percentage of GDP decreased despite sizable primary deficits on account of a combination of high growth and negative real interest

rates. The debt dynamics reversed in 1994, when the restrictive monetary policy stance implied by the exchange-rate-based nominal anchor policy reduced inflation to single-digit rates, which, in turn, led to positive growth-adjusted real interest rates on the public debt. Thus, while the interest rate dynamics and the deficit-related flows had offsetting effects on the overall debt dynamics in 1991–93, they both contributed to an increase in the debt-to-GDP ratio in 1994–97.

Reflecting considerable political and macroeconomic uncertainties immediately after the war, Lebanon initially had only very limited access to ei-

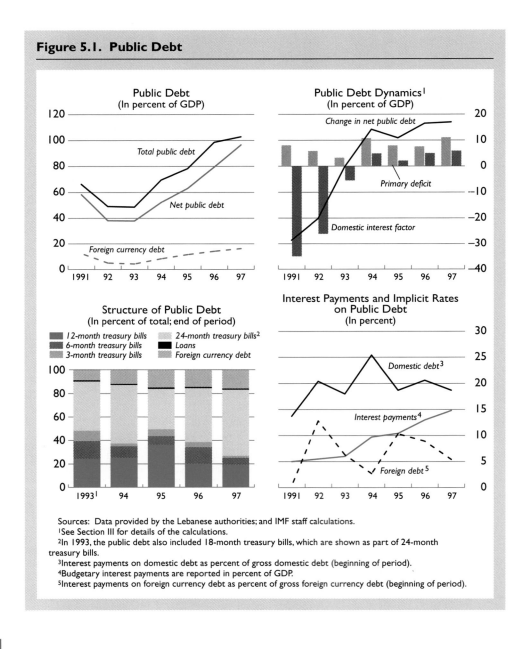

Figure 5.1. Public Debt

Sources: Data provided by the Lebanese authorities; and IMF staff calculations.
[1]See Section III for details of the calculations.
[2]In 1993, the public debt also included 18-month treasury bills, which are shown as part of 24-month treasury bills.
[3]Interest payments on domestic debt as percent of gross domestic debt (beginning of period).
[4]Budgetary interest payments are reported in percent of GDP.
[5]Interest payments on foreign currency debt as percent of gross foreign currency debt (beginning of period).

ther international capital markets or foreign official financing and had to resort to domestic capital markets to finance its budget deficit. Short-term treasury bills denominated in Lebanese pounds with maturities from 3 to 12 months were the only available instrument. In mid-1991, the authorities also started issuing 24-month treasury bonds with semiannual coupon payments. For a while, treasury bills with a maturity of 18 months were also available, but their issue was discontinued given the limited interest by the investor community. Reflecting these developments, Lebanon's debt structure has been characterized by a high, albeit gradually declining share of short-term, treasury bills denominated in Lebanese pounds in total public debt (Table 5.1). Increasingly, 24-month treasury bonds have become the dominant Lebanese pound debt instrument and have, on average, accounted for 53 percent of all outstanding treasury bills and bonds during 1993–97.[2] Nevertheless, given an uneven distribution of new issues and a strong tendency for the bunching of new issues at peak dates, the effective maturity of the outstanding treasury bills and bonds has on average been only about 9–10 months.[3]

Except for episodes during which substantial pressures on the exchange rate peg emerged (see below), the central bank has generally refrained from budgetary financing. Accordingly, most treasury bills have been held by commercial banks and nonbank private entities.[4] Treasury bills have been the main short-term, Lebanese pound assets in Lebanese financial markets, and, given the role of commercial banks as the principal intermediaries, are the main determinants of quasi-monetary Lebanese pound liabilities. Treasury bill holdings by the nonbank entities have been increasing, in particular since 1995. This change in the structure of treasury bill holdings has been attributed to the staggering interest rate setting by commercial banks and the deepening of financial markets. The latter has allowed for a larger investor base, including foreign, that is, nonresident, investors. At the end of 1997, about 7 percent of the outstanding treasury bills were held by nonresident investors.

Foreign currency debt, as a share of GDP, was relatively low during 1991–93, but started to increase since 1994. Initially, the foreign currency debt was largely composed of debt owed to commercial banks and to bilateral official creditors. Since 1994, however, the Lebanese government has also been able to tap international capital markets for budgetary financing: seven Eurobonds denominated in U.S. dollars and one bond in deutsche mark (issued in the local German financial market), for a total face value of about $2.4 billion, have been issued.[5] The issue of foreign currency debt is subject to parliamentary approval. In 1994, the Lebanese parliament approved foreign currency borrowing by the central government in international capital markets up to a limit of $1 billion.[6] In January 1998, the parliament approved additional foreign currency borrowing of $2 billion. Foreign currency borrowing for reconstruction does not fall in this category as the parliament has approved most projects, including their foreign financing part, as part of a multiyear expenditure program rather than on a year-by-year basis.[7]

The foreign currency debt has been characterized by an average effective maturity that is significantly longer than that of the domestic currency debt. The foreign loans contracted by the Council for Development and Reconstruction (CDR), the government agency in charge of the reconstruction program, have maturities of 10 years and more and are typically concessional with a significant grant element and a grace period. The maturity of the international bonds issued by Lebanon has also increased. While the first Eurobond issued in 1994 had a maturity of three years, more recent bond issues have maturities of up to 10 years.

The large public debt, in the context of the overall macroeconomic policy mix (see below), has also led to a substantial interest rate burden on the budget. In 1991, interest payments amounted to 17 percent of expenditure (5 percent of GDP). Since then, they have been gradually increasing, and amounted to 35 percent of expenditure in 1997 (15 percent of GDP). A striking aspect of the interest rate costs is the differential between the interest rate costs incurred on Lebanese pound debt and on foreign currency debt

---

[2]The decomposition of treasury bills and bonds into maturities reported in Table 5.1 is based on the maturity of the bills at the time of issue and not on the remaining time to maturity.

[3]Treasury bills and bonds are referred to as treasury bills in the remainder of the paper.

[4]The latter category also includes public entities that are not included in the budget (e.g., social security fund), which hold their excess cash balances in treasury bills. These holdings amounted to about 5 percent of all outstanding treasury bills and bonds during recent years.

[5]In October 1994, Lebanon issued a three-year Eurobond for US$400 million. In July 1995, a five-year $300 million Eurobond followed. In May 1996, the government issued a 51-month Eurobond for $100 million. In May and June 1997, respectively, a five-year deutsche mark bond of DM 250 million and a 10-year Yankee bond of $100 million were issued. In October 1997, the redemption of the 1993 Eurobond was refinanced with a 10-year Eurobonds of $4000 million. In April 1998, two $500 million Eurobonds with maturities of three- and five-years, respectively, were issued.

[6]The 1997 $100 million Yankee bond, which was issued by Lebanon on behalf of the electricity company Electricité du Liban, does not fall under this limit.

[7]In the central government budget submitted to parliament, only the domestic counterpart financing of the reconstruction program is included.

Table 5.1. Public Debt Structure

	1991	1992	1993	1994	1995	1996	1997
	(In billions of Lebanese pounds; end of period)						
Gross public debt	2,737	4,651	6,363	10,619	14,079	20,109	23,504
Gross domestic public debt	2,230	4,178	5,804	9,348	11,997	17,229	19,787
By instrument							
Treasury bills and bonds[1]	2,015	4,018	5,739	9,266	11,838	17,022	19,578
Long-term treasury bonds	328	1,236	2,592	5,292	4,873	9,264	13,271
Twenty-four-month bonds	328	1,200	2,520	5,020	4,644	8,835	12,430
Accrued interest	0	36	72	272	230	429	580
Short-term treasury bills	1,687	2,782	3,147	3,974	6,965	7,759	6,307
Twelve-month bills	1,247	1,112	1,600	2,687	5,129	4,103	4,618
Six-month bills	275	690	964	1,024	987	2,762	1,270
Three-month bills	165	980	583	262	850	893	419
Loans	215	160	65	82	159	207	209
By holder							
Banque du Liban	276	284	454	105	195	124	375
Treasury bills	68	139	392	27	92	24	274
Other	208	145	62	78	103	100	101
Commercial banks and financial institutions	1,548	3,099	4,245	7,345	8,453	12,638	13,532
Treasury bills	1,302	3,083	4,242	7,341	8,397	12,532	13,424
Other	7	16	3	4	57	106	109
Nonbank private and other (treasury bills)	644	796	1,105	1,898	3,349	4,467	5,880
Gross external public debt[2]	507	473	560	1,271	2,082	2,881	3,717
Public sector deposits	329	1,034	1,389	2,636	2,710	3,871	1,406
Net public debt[3]	2,408	3,618	4,974	7,983	11,369	16,239	22,098
	(In percent of gross public debt)						
Gross public debt	100.0	100.0	100.0	100.0	100.0	100.0	100.0
Gross domestic public debt	81.5	89.8	91.2	88.0	85.2	85.7	84.2
By instrument							
Treasury bills and bonds[1]	73.6	86.4	90.2	87.3	84.1	84.6	83.3
Long-term treasury-bonds	12.0	26.6	40.7	49.8	34.6	46.1	56.5
Twenty-four-month bonds	12.0	25.8	39.6	47.3	33.0	43.9	52.9
Accrued interest	0.0	0.8	1.1	2.6	1.6	2.1	2.5
Short-term treasury bills	61.6	59.8	49.5	37.4	49.5	38.6	26.8
Twelve-month bills	45.5	23.9	25.1	25.3	36.4	20.4	19.6
Six-month bills	10.0	14.8	15.1	9.6	7.0	13.7	5.4
Three-month bills	6.0	21.1	9.2	2.5	6.0	4.4	1.8
Loans	7.9	3.4	1.0	0.8	1.1	1.0	0.9
By holder							
Banque du Liban	10.1	6.1	7.1	1.0	1.4	0.6	1.6
Treasury bills	2.5	3.0	6.2	0.3	0.7	0.1	1.2
Other	7.6	3.1	1.0	0.7	0.7	0.5	0.4
Commercial banks and financial institutions	56.6	66.6	66.7	69.2	60.0	62.8	57.6
Treasury bills	47.6	66.3	66.7	69.1	59.6	62.3	57.1
Other	0.3	0.3	0.1	0.0	0.4	0.5	0.5
Nonbank private and other (treasury bills)	23.5	17.1	17.4	17.9	23.8	22.2	25.0
Gross external public debt[2]	18.5	10.2	8.8	12.0	14.8	14.3	15.8
Public sector deposits	12.0	22.2	21.8	24.8	19.2	19.2	6.0
Net public debt[3]	88.0	77.8	78.2	75.2	80.8	80.8	94.0
Memorandum item							
GDP (in billions of Lebanese pounds)	4,132	9,499	13,122	15,305	18,028	20,417	22,878

Sources: Banque du Liban; IMF, *International Financial Statistics*; and IMF staff estimates.
[1]Face value of the outstanding treasury bills, including accrued interest on 24-month treasury bonds.
[2]The stock of external public debt is valued at the end-of-period exchange rate.
[3]Defined as gross public debt minus public sector deposits with the banking system.

(Figure 5.1). Foreign currency debt has been associated with much more favorable terms since 1993, reflecting not only the grant element in some official financing, but also the low interest rates on international bonds issued by Lebanon relative to debt instruments in Lebanese pounds. Since the first issue in 1994, the yield spread relative to comparable U.S. government bonds and bills has decreased considerably despite the lengthening of maturities, reflecting in part increased awareness about Lebanon by foreign investors, but also the large foreign exchange reserves and the high reconstruction-related growth, which have been perceived favorably in capital markets. Lebanese pound assets, however, have been associated with high nominal and real interest rates, as indicated by the substantial interest differentials between Lebanese pound and comparable U.S. dollar assets (Figure 5.2).

Public Debt, Monetary Policy, and Interest Rate Dynamics

The authorities have given a high priority to prudent monetary policy, taking into account the constraints imposed by the high dollarization in domestic asset markets, the virtually unlimited capital

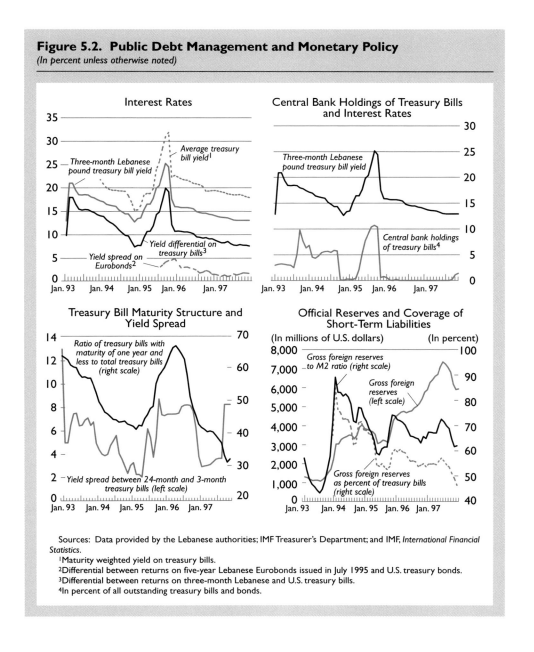

Figure 5.2. Public Debt Management and Monetary Policy
(In percent unless otherwise noted)

Sources: Data provided by the Lebanese authorities; IMF Treasurer's Department; and IMF, *International Financial Statistics.*
[1]Maturity weighted yield on treasury bills.
[2]Differential between returns on five-year Lebanese Eurobonds issued in July 1995 and U.S. treasury bonds.
[3]Differential between returns on three-month Lebanese and U.S. treasury bills.
[4]In percent of all outstanding treasury bills and bonds.

mobility, and the difficult macroeconomic situation, characterized by large budget and current account deficits, and a large stock of short-term public debt, all in an environment of domestic and regional uncertainty. In the circumstances, flexible and high interest rates were required to ensure both the inflow of capital and increases in the share of Lebanese pound assets in the portfolios of domestic investors. Demand by the latter has been characterized by a high substitutability between Lebanese pound and U.S. dollar assets, particularly during the early years of reconstruction. The prudent policy stance has been reflected in the strong cushion of gross official foreign exchange reserves that has been accumulated since late 1992. This cushion has been crucial in signaling the authorities' commitment to their exchange rate policy, but has also allowed for some limited interest rate smoothing.

During 1993–97, monetary policy considerations have dominated public debt management. Given the paramount position of commercial banks in the intermediation of treasury bills (through their balance sheet), the interest rates in the primary markets for treasury bills and bonds have been the main instruments to control Lebanese pound liquidity. Moreover, in view of their role as primary vehicle for channeling foreign exchange inflows into Lebanese pound assets, treasury bills have also been instrumental in allowing the central bank to achieve a satisfactory coverage of monetary and quasi-monetary Lebanese pound liabilities by foreign exchange reserves. Accordingly, the issue of treasury bills over and above budgetary financing needs in times of favorable financial market sentiments has enabled the authorities to build up the desired cushion of foreign exchange reserves. These sterilization operations, which are reflected in the public sector deposits at the central bank, have at times led to a significant divergence between gross and net public debt.

With the normalization of economic activity and the achievements in nominal stabilization, the central bank was able to gradually reduce the nominal interest rate in the primary sales of treasury bills between mid-1993 and mid-1997. This general decline was interrupted by episodes of heightened political uncertainty, which led to pressures on the exchange rate peg and the foreign exchange reserves. During such episodes, the demand for treasury bills in the primary sales was typically lower than the supply, and the central bank had to temporarily cover the deficit, deviating from its general policy of refraining from budgetary financing, or the government ran down its deposits, or both. Furthermore, to maintain the de facto currency peg, the central bank had to raise Lebanese pound interest rates in the primary sales to avoid an inflationary expansion of Lebanese pound liquidity and large reserve losses. As shown in

Figure 5.2, the three-month treasury bill yield, the three-month interest differential with respect to U.S. treasury bills, and the share of central bank holdings in total treasury bill holdings are closely related because of this interaction of monetary policy and debt management.

The treasury bill maturity structure in Lebanon, with an effective maturity of typically less than one year, reinforced the problems during episodes of heightened political uncertainty because of the large proportion of government debt that had to be refinanced continuously. At the same time, investors revealed a strong preference for treasury bills with very short maturities, with important implications for the effective maturity of the outstanding stock of Lebanese pound debt. Therefore, the authorities have pursued a policy of increasing the maturity structure of government debt denominated in Lebanese pounds whenever financial market conditions allowed for such a move without excessive budgetary costs. Moreover, during and after such episodes of financial market pressures, the central bank also used swap operations in the secondary market for treasury bills to smooth its maturity profile so as to avoid the refinancing of large amounts of maturing treasury bills at certain peak dates.

In the second half of 1997 and the first four months of 1998, following the developments in Asian financial markets, an intensification of the hostilities in Lebanon's south, and the widely publicized news about unfavorable budgetary and public debt developments, the Lebanese authorities had once again to deal with unfavorable market sentiments and difficulties in rolling over maturing Lebanese pound treasury bills. Dollarization reversed and started to rise while the central bank began losing foreign exchange reserves. Given the significantly higher debt level and the related budgetary burden, the authorities decided to use a different strategy to cope with the financial market pressures. First, they signaled their intention to address the fiscal problems by incorporating frontloaded adjustment in the 1998 budget (see Section III). Second, they limited reserve losses and dollarization through shifting the slope of the secondary market yield curve for Lebanese pound treasury bills rather than raising the primary market yield curve level as in 1995. This rise in the slope was accomplished by swapping in the secondary market maturing treasury bills and newly issued, short-term treasury bills held by banks and the (nonfinancial) public against newly issued longer-term 12- and 24-month bills at a discount. The burden associated with the positive swap rates (difference between secondary and primary market yields on longer-term treasury bills) was born by the central bank. As shown in Figure 5.2, the sharp increase in the secondary market yield spread was effective in reducing the short-term Lebanese pound liquidity in the form of short-term treasury bills. However, with the larger amount of short-term Lebanese pound liquidity in the system, the reserve losses were considerably larger than in 1995. In May 1998, the financial market pressures finally eased following the encouraging budgetary outcome of the first four months and the successful mobilization of external financing, including through the issue of two Eurobonds for a total of $1 billion in the beginning of April.

Institutional Aspects of Public Debt Management

While the primary responsibility for public debt management falls in the domain of the ministry of finance, the central bank has had the operational responsibility for debt denominated in Lebanese pounds. The CDR is entrusted with the acquisition of foreign currency loans related to reconstruction projects. The central bank runs the weekly treasury bill auctions, with interest rates being set in consultation with the ministry of finance. Since 1994, all treasury bills and bonds are issued in auctions. Commercial banks are allowed to place both competitive bids and noncompetitive bids on behalf of customers, while other participants are allowed to place noncompetitive bids, which are being served at the average yield resulting from the competitive bids.

Theoretical Aspects of Public Debt Management

In his seminal study on debt-management policy, Tobin (1963) asserted that "minimum cost for required economic impact" is the proper criterion for an optimal debt management policy and identified the key issue in public debt management as: "How are long-run interest costs on a given volume of federal debt to be minimized, given the contribution that debt management and monetary policy jointly make to economic stabilization?" The economics profession has since greatly changed the mainstream view about the role, capability, and desirability of an active stabilization policy by governments. Nevertheless, Tobin's criterion has remained highly relevant, albeit with a different emphasis on the role of monetary policy in stabilization policy and the primary purpose of optimizing the structure of public debt.[8]

In the following summary, the focus lies on three policy objectives that have important ramifications for public debt management: tax smoothing, credibility of macroeconomic policies, and short-term stabilization policy.

Tax Smoothing

Barro (1979) pointed out that it is optimal, from a welfare point of view, to smooth tax rates across time if they have a distortionary effect either on the labor-leisure choice or on the intertemporal allocation of savings.[9] If they do, governments should issue debt in periods during which the tax base (growth) is lower than on average and repay debt in periods during which the tax base (growth) is higher than on average. Optimal debt management under these circumstances would aim at minimizing the debt-servicing costs by issuing debt instruments, which imply debt-service payments that are positively correlated with the primary balance. In this regard, it has been pointed out that, if GDP is negatively correlated with expenditure growth and is positively correlated with revenue growth, the returns on government liabilities should be made contingent on GDP growth. In practice, debt instruments with returns tied to GDP developments have not yet been introduced.

Credibility

The structure of public debt has important implications for the credibility of a government's macroeconomic policies as the literature on time-consistency and inconsistency problems has shown. A diversified public debt structure is often desirable because it reduces the incentives that the government has in reducing the real value of its debt service and thereby lowers the required return. The diversity encompasses the dimensions of maturity, indexation, and currency denomination. Changes in the structure of public debt can become policy instruments because they send important signals to financial markets.

Credibility and time-consistency issues arise because of the government's ex post incentive to renege on its commitment to repaying the debt. For example, if taxation is distortionary and if increases in the tax rate have political costs, the government has an incentive to change its commitment ex post.[10] In-

---

[8]For example, a 1995 report by the Treasury of the United Kingdom on the Debt Management Review identified the objective of the debt management policy as follows: "to minimize over the long term the costs of meeting the Government's financing needs, taking account of risk, whilst ensuring that debt management policy is consistent with monetary policy" (p. 3). This objective is not very different from the objective put forward by Tobin.

[9]See also Barro (1995).

[10]For real bonds, the prominent examples of such changes in commitment are outright default on debt or a capital levy. See Eichengreen (1990) on capital levies in theory and practice.

vestors, however, recognize the government's ex post incentives to renege on its obligations and will either ask for high premiums or refuse to buy government debt all together, an outcome that is suboptimal compared with the outcome when a government is able to credibly commit itself to abstain from reneging. Institutional constraints and reputation have served as mechanisms to avoid such problems in practice. An interesting mechanism to avoid time-inconsistency problems was proposed by Lucas and Stokey (1983), who showed that through issuing bonds with different maturities the government can tie its hands to avoid the temptation of reneging on its obligations.[11]

This time-inconsistency problem becomes even more relevant for nominal debt. In this case, the government can reduce the real tax burden arising from its commitments to service the outstanding debt by staging a surprise rise in the price level or, in other words, by monetizing the debt. Again, investors, recognize these ex post incentives for monetization and will ask for risk premiums that will compensate for inflation-induced losses. As pointed out by Persson, Persson, and Svensson (1987), who extended the result of Lucas and Stokey to monetary models, the maturity structure of the nominal public debt can again be an important instrument in reducing time-inconsistency problems, provided that increasing inflation (price level increases) is a costly policy option for the government.[12] Under the latter condition, the incentives to monetize are negatively correlated with the maturity structure of public debt: the shorter is the average maturity, the larger is the price level increase within a period that is needed to reduce the real burden of servicing the debt.

The maturity structure of the nominal public debt in local currency is only one dimension in the optimization of structure of public debt. Two other important dimensions concern the relative share of nominal and real (price index linked) debt and the relative share of foreign currency debt. By and large, the optimization along these dimensions is also related to minimizing problems of time inconsistency, albeit through different channels. For example, as pointed out by Bohn (1990b) and Watanabe (1992), if purchasing power parity does not hold, foreign currency debt reduces the government's incentives to monetize the debt-servicing obligations through exchange rate adjustments.

Credibility and reputation, which are gained over time, are important mechanisms to enhance the government's role in economic policies in addition to instruments of public debt management, such as the structure of the public debt. There is, of course, an eminent relationship between credibility and public debt management since the latter can be an important signaling device when a government tries to establish its reputation or when it comes to stabilizing general public expectations. This last point is particularly relevant if self-fulfilling expectations can lead to multiple equilibriums, including "good" and "bad" ones. Signaling can be important in increasing the probability that a good equilibrium materializes. In the case of nominal debt, for example, increasing the share of indexed debt can be an important device in this respect.[13]

The problem of self-fulfilling expectations related to the nominal public debt has also been investigated in the context of fixed exchange rate regimes.[14] If the public expects a devaluation, the government would have to raise interest rates to defend the peg. Doing so will increase the burden of servicing the nominal public debt, and if taxation is a costly option for the government, the government might be forced into a devaluation or depreciation to monetize its debt-service obligations. Foreign currency debt can become an important signaling or credibility device under such circumstances. Similarly, Alesina, Prati, and Tabellini (1990) and Giavazzi and Pagano (1990) identified the special role of short-term debt in this context. If the share of short-term debt in the total public debt is very high, it can reinforce the expectations that the government will not use interest rates to defend the currency. Accordingly, they recommend a more balanced maturity structure.

Short-Term Stabilization

Changes in the maturity structure of public debt have also been proposed as an instrument for an activist stabilization policy.[15] If short-term and long-term bonds are imperfect substitutes, the central bank or the debt-management authority can use changes in the maturity structure of the domestic currency debt to change the yield curve, which in turn can affect economic activity. For example, Friedman (1992) argues that a change to a shorter maturity structure can invert the yield curve for government bonds. If long-

---

[11]To be precise, Lucas and Stokey showed that there exist maturity structures for the outstanding public debt such that the government has no incentive to deviate from the optimal plan given by the precommitment plan at any time. The latter plan is the one that would materialize if the government could credibly commit itself, that is, a plan under which the government would not renege on its debt obligations.

[12]Persson, Persson, and Svensson (1987) use a model with complete financial markets. Calvo and Guidotti (1990a, 1990b, 1992), in a series of papers, explore the implications of incomplete financial markets.

[13]See Calvo (1988) for details.
[14]See Obstfeld (1986, 1994, 1995) in particular.
[15]See, among others, Tobin (1963, 1969) and Friedman (1992).

term bonds and equity are closer substitutes than short-term bonds and equity, the shift will stimulate the demand for equity capital and thus for investment, which in turn will stimulate economic activity. Following trends in mainstream macroeconomics, many authors have expressed doubts about the feasibility of using public debt management as an instrument for stabilization. Empirical evidence on the substitutability among various assets is still scarce, and it is not clear whether this instrument is robust with respect to forward-looking expectations in financial markets. In many countries, the use of debt management as a stabilization policy tool is also infeasible because financial markets lack the depth for these policies to be effective.

Public Debt Management: Options and Strategies

Lebanon's outstanding public debt, whether measured in gross or net terms, is sizable, and the corresponding interest payments are the largest expenditure item in the budget. Following the literature, the general objective of public debt management should be to arrange the public debt structure so as to minimize the medium-term, risk-adjusted costs of overall public debt in a way that is consistent with monetary policy objectives. The greater access to international financial markets and the deepening of domestic financial markets in recent years have increased the scope for enhancing the strategy for public debt management.

In the following exposition, the issue of the optimal debt structure will be examined in light of the goal of minimizing the risk-adjusted costs of the public debt, taking into account the macroeconomic environment of the last few years. The discussion is qualitative rather than quantitative since neither a full-fledged macroeconometric model nor econometric estimates related to key behavioral relationships are yet available to determine quantitative benchmarks for the public debt structure. Given the important linkages with monetary policy during the period 1993–97, the issue of the consistency of public debt management with monetary policy objectives will also be reviewed.

Minimizing Risk-Adjusted Costs

The risk-adjusted cost of the public debt is a medium- to long-term concept. The risks involved in maintaining a particular debt structure are related to future price or interest rate changes resulting from shocks to the economy. In the determination of these risks, the planned policy responses to such shocks should also be taken into account.

In the assessment of the current debt structure with regard to its risk-adjusted costs, it is useful for discussion, to evaluate the issues of minimizing the level and the risks of the interest rate costs separately. Given sizable Lebanese pound–U.S. dollar interest rate differentials and the slope of the Lebanese pound yield curve, minimizing the level of interest rate costs would mean increasing the shares of three- and six-month Lebanese pound treasury bills in the total amount of treasury bills outstanding, and substantially raising the share of foreign currency debt in total public debt (Figure 5.2). The recent experience with foreign currency debt suggests that reducing the interest rate costs has been consistent with the simultaneous lengthening of the maturity structure given the recent declines in interest spreads with government assets denominated in U.S. dollars. Regarding Lebanese pound debt, the minimization of the level of interest rate costs is inconsistent with the lengthening of the maturity structure, given the slope of the Lebanese pound treasury bill yield curve. The trade-off between lowering the interest rate costs and the lengthening of the Lebanese pound debt maturity structure is even more significant once the potential for further downward shifts in the yield curve is taken into account. Such shifts would result from the declining inflation differential with partner countries and the envisaged fiscal adjustment over the next two to three years.

A reorientation of the public debt structure toward increasing the shares of foreign currency debt and very short-term Lebanese pound treasury bills in total debt to reduce costs bears obvious risks given the current macroeconomic environment in Lebanon. Three risks appear to be particularly relevant in the current circumstances: the foreign interest rate risk, the confidence risk, and the exchange rate risk.

Increases in foreign short-term interest rates pose a significant risk in light of the substantial capital inflows into Lebanon. It is unlikely, however, that a particular debt structure could reduce or amplify the risk-adjusted costs since such an increase would shift the entire Lebanese pound yield curve through interest rate parity arbitrage (up to a risk premium) and would also be reflected in the interest rate costs on foreign currency debt. Changes in foreign interest rates have a direct effect on interest rate costs, as well as indirect effects through reversals in capital flows as demonstrated by episodes in the early 1990s and in 1994. These indirect risks have similar implications to those of the confidence risks.

Changes in financial market sentiments pose significant risk given the large budget deficits and the sizable external current account deficit, in the context of the exchange-rate-based nominal anchor policy and a high degree of capital mobility. The impact of changes in market sentiments on domestic interest rate levels is likely to be similar in nature to the case of changes in foreign interest rates, since the central bank would have to raise interest rates to defend the exchange rate peg. The interest rate risk implied by such changes could be considerably larger, however, since an intense speculative dynamics fueled by the large short-term debt maturing during such an episode could develop. Many episodes have shown that high and volatile domestic currency interest rates are needed to maintain nominal exchange rate stability and to refinance short-term public debt during times of turmoil in financial markets. As argued earlier, a diversified public debt structure is likely to mitigate the effect of such a shock on the medium-term, risk-adjusted costs, while a public debt structure with a large share of short-term debt is likely to amplify it. The general increases of the share of 24-month treasury bonds in the stock of outstanding treasury bills over the period 1991–97 and the share of foreign debt with longer maturities in the total debt have reflected the Lebanese authorities' intention to reduce the risk associated with the short-term public debt denominated in Lebanese pounds, even though this prudent policy stance has been associated with considerable budgetary costs until now. The general decline in the slope of the Lebanese pound yield curve observed in 1996 mitigated the effects of the lengthening of the debt structure on the level of interest rate costs in 1997.

A policy leading to a substantial increase in the share of foreign currency debt in total debt must take the risk of future exchange rate changes into account. Assessing the risk-adjusted interest rate costs of foreign debt without taking into account this risk implies a downward bias in the risk-adjusted costs.

In view of the various trade-offs, a dilemma confronts public debt management in Lebanon. The current public debt structure, characterized by a large share of domestic currency debt with an effective maturity of the Lebanese pound debt of less than one year, is uncomfortable given the level of debt; however, any attempt to lengthen the debt maturity structure is likely to have substantial budgetary implications. Nevertheless, the continued reduction of the medium-term risks associated with the public debt should remain one of the operational goals of public debt management in the near future to safeguard the achievements in macroeconomic stabilization. A two-phased approach could be the appropriate policy response to this dilemma. In a first step, the maturity structure could be lengthened by slightly increasing the share of foreign currency. In a second step, in connection with a strong fiscal adjustment package, the structure of public debt denominated in Lebanese pounds, particularly with respect to the maturity profile, could be enhanced with relatively

lower budgetary costs. By asking the parliament to approve the issuance of another $2 billion of foreign currency debt in conjunction with the 1998 budget, the government has opted for this approach.

Monetary Policy and Public Debt Management

During 1993–97, the Lebanese authorities succeeded in establishing the credibility of their commitment toward price and exchange rate stability. Close coordination of monetary policy and public debt management has been key to the success. In the process, the minimization of the risks associated with the short-term public debt through a sufficient reserve coverage has been given priority relative to the minimization of the level of the interest rate costs.

The gradual deepening of Lebanon's financial markets in recent years has allowed the central bank to create its own instruments (certificates of deposit for 45 and 60 days) that can be used for monetary policy. Nevertheless, interest rates on treasury bills are likely to remain the most important monetary policy instruments for some time given the large outstanding stock of domestic currency debt and its implication for short-term domestic currency liquidity.[16] In the context of the exchange-rate-based nominal anchor policy, monetary policy will continue to be geared toward ensuring the exchange rate peg while maintaining reserves at prudent levels. From this perspective, the reduction of the risk-adjusted interest rate costs of public debt through a further diversification of the public debt structure will also be appropriate since it will contribute to foster the credibility of monetary policy through the mechanisms summarized earlier, in particular, by reducing the constraints imposed by the short duration of the domestic debt.

Conclusions

The authorities have succeeded in managing a large and growing stock of short-term public debt under difficult macroeconomic conditions. A prudent monetary policy, which has been carefully coordinated with public debt management, has been key to this success. In the early years of reconstruction, public debt management was constrained by the limited access to international capital markets

---

[16]In fact, some authors favor governmental securities relative to central bank securities for open market operations (e.g., Quintyn, 1996), since the former can better "serve as catalysts in financial market development," and their markets are typically more liquid.

and by the few available domestic currency debt instruments, features which have been in part associated with macroeconomic uncertainty. The recent progress in nominal stabilization has opened the door for enhancing public debt management.

Over the next few years, public debt management in Lebanon will be essential in supporting overall macroeconomic policies and reducing the burden on monetary policy. To this end, it should primarily aim at lengthening the maturity structure of domestic public debt, which is essentially short term, thereby reducing the vulnerability to financial market sentiments and shocks. However, given the current level of short-term interest rates, the current slope of the yield curve, and the potential for a general interest rate decline in the future, the authorities face a trade-off between reducing the budgetary costs and the risks associated with the current structure of the domestic currency debt. While some debt instruments, for example, floating rate notes, would allow for lengthening the maturity structure without being locked in at the current high interest rates, significant further progress in lengthening the maturity structure will depend critically on fiscal adjustment and the related decline in nominal and real domestic currency interest rates.

Lengthening the average maturity of the outstanding domestic currency debt will also depend on the progress in deepening and widening financial markets. Two factors are crucial in this regard. First, the fiscal consolidation envisaged by the authorities will contribute to increased macroeconomic stability and investor confidence and will thus raise the demand for medium- and long-term Lebanese pound government papers. Second, the development of liquid secondary securities markets is essential. With longer maturities, investors would need to be certain that their short-term liquidity needs can be met even if they hold medium- and long-term government securities. While the regulatory and organizational framework (including clearing and settlement procedures) has been put in place (see Section VI), secondary market activities have nevertheless remained limited so far, mainly due to the current short, average effective maturity of the Lebanese pound debt and the frequent (weekly) treasury bill auctions. In the future, issuing Lebanese pound treasury bills and bonds with longer maturities might be sufficient to activate secondary market activities. Reducing the frequency of treasury bill auctions could provide additional support.

The recent strengthening of budgetary control and planning procedures will also facilitate the projection of the financing needs of the government, thereby allowing for a longer planning horizon in public debt management. This could enable the authorities to consider enhancing the credibility of public debt management through changes in the institutional set up. Measures could focus on increasing transparency by the public announcement of the goals and benchmarks for public debt management and on the creation of an independent public debt management agency. Such an agency would be given the mandate to manage public debt within the parameters set by monetary and fiscal policy, thereby reducing potential conflicts between monetary policy and public debt management.

References

Alesina, Alberto, Alessandro Prati, and Guido Tabellini, 1990, "Public Confidence and Debt Management: A Model and Case Study of Italy," in *Public Debt Management: Theory and History,* 1990, ed. by Rudiger Dornbusch and Mario Draghi (Cambridge; New York: Cambridge University Press), pp. 94–117.

Barro, Robert J., 1979, "On the Determination of the Public Debt," *Journal of Political Economy,* Vol. 87 (October), pp. 940–71.

———, 1995, "Optimal Debt Management," NBER Working Paper No. 5327 (Cambridge, Massachusetts: National Bureau of Economic Research).

Blanchard, Olivier J., and Alessandro Missale, 1994, "Debt Burden and Debt Maturity," *American Economic Review,* Vol. 84 (March), pp. 309–19.

Bohn, Henning, 1988, "Why Do We Have Nominal Government Debt?" *Journal of Monetary Economics,* Vol. 21 (January), pp. 127–40.

———, 1990a, "Tax Smoothing with Financial Instruments," *American Economic Review,* Vol. 80 (December), pp. 1217–30.

———, 1990b, "A Positive Theory of Foreign Currency Debt," *Journal of International Economics,* Vol. 29 (April), pp. 273–92.

Calvo, Guillermo A., 1988, "Servicing the Public Debt: The Role of Expectations," *American Economic Review,* Vol. 78 (September), pp. 647–61.

———, and Pablo E. Guidotti, 1990a, "Credibility and Nominal Debt: Exploring the Role of Maturity in Managing Inflation," *Staff Papers,* International Monetary Fund, Vol. 37 (September), pp. 612–35.

———, 1990b, "Management of the Nominal Public Debt: Theory and Applications," IMF Working Paper 90/115 (Washington: International Monetary Fund).

———, 1992, "Optimal Maturity of Nominal Government Debt: An Infinite-Horizon Model," *International Economic Review,* Vol. 33 (November), pp. 895–919.

Eichengreen, Barry, 1990, "The Capital Levy in Theory and Practice," in *Public Debt Management: Theory and History,* 1990, ed. by Rudiger Dornbusch and Mario Draghi (Cambridge; New York: Cambridge University Press), pp. 191–220.

Friedman, Benjamin M., 1992, "Debt Management, Interest Rates, and Economic Activity," in *Does Debt Management Matter?* by Jonas Agell, Mats Persson, and Benjamin M. Friedman (Oxford: Clarendon Press), pp. 109–40.

Giavazzi, Francesco and Marco Pagano, 1990, "Confidence Crisis and Public Debt Management," in *Public Debt Management: Theory and History, 1990,* ed. by Rudiger Dornbusch and Mario Draghi (Cambridge; New York: Cambridge University Press), pp. 125–142.

Lucas, Robert E. Jr., and Nancy L. Stokey 1983, "Optimal Fiscal and Monetary Policy in an Economy Without Capital," *Journal of Monetary Economics,* Vol. 12 (July), pp. 55–94.

Obstfeld, Maurice, 1986, "Rational and Self-Fulfilling Balance of Payments Crises," *American Economic Review,* Vol. 76 (March), pp. 72–81.

———, 1994, "The Logic of Currency Crises," NBER Working Paper No. 4640 (Cambridge, Massachusetts: National Bureau of Economic Research).

———, 1995, "Models of Currency Crises with Self-Fulfilling Features," NBER Working Paper No. 5285 (Cambridge, Massachusetts: National Bureau of Economic Research.

Persson, Mats, Torsten Persson, and Lars E.O. Svensson, 1987, "Time Consistency of Fiscal and Monetary Policy," *Econometrica,* Vol. 55 (November), pp. 1419–32.

Quintyn, Marc, 1996, "Government Securities Versus Central Bank Securities in Developing Market-Based Monetary Operations," in *Coordination of Monetary and Public Debt Management: Design and Management of Operational Arrangements,* ed. by Venkataraman Sundararajan, Hans Blommestein, and Peter Dattels (Washington: International Monetary Fund).

Swaroop, Vinaya, 1994, "The Public Finance of Infrastructure Projects: Issues and Options," Policy Research Working Paper No. 1288 (Washington: World Bank, Policy Research Department).

Swedish Ministry of Finance, 1997, "Statsskuldspolitiken" (Public Debt Management, summary in English), Final report of the Public Debt Management committee, SOU 1997:66 (Stockholm: Ministry of Finance).

Tobin, James, 1963, "An Essay on Principles of Debt Management," in *Commission on Money and Credit, Fiscal and Debt Management Policies,* (Englewood Cliffs, N.J.: Prentice-Hall). Reprinted in Tobin, James, 1971, *Essays in Economics,* Vol. 1 (Amsterdam: North-Holland), pp. 378–445.

———, 1969, "A General Equilibrium Approach to Monetary Theory," *Journal of Money, Credit, and Banking,* Vol. 1 (March), pp. 15–29.

U.K. Treasury, 1995, *Report of the Debt Management Review* (London: Publishing Unit, HM Treasury).

Watanabe, Tsutomu, 1992, "The Optimal Currency Composition of Government Debt," *Bank of Japan Monetary and Economic Studies,* Vol. 10 (November), pp. 31–62 .

VI Financial Sector Developments

Klaus Enders

Lebanon has traditionally played an important role as a regional service center for the Middle East, notably in tourism, financial services, trade-related services, and publishing.[1] This role was based on Lebanon's location, a tradition of an open and liberal market-based economic system (including a long-standing bank secrecy law, liberal rights of establishment, and the virtual absence of any control on current or capital account transactions) and a strong human capital base derived from an efficient (and largely private) education system. Taxation has generally been low and most interest earnings are tax exempt. The large Lebanese community abroad has maintained solid ties with Lebanon, reflected, inter alia, in a persistent high level of capital inflows and transfers, and repatriation of knowledge.

The civil war years brought massive destruction of physical infrastructure and losses of human capital, including through emigration. Other financial centers in the Middle East partly took over Beirut's traditional role as uncertainty, destruction, and the severance of traditional ties affected the ability of the financial system to function and adapt to the new technologies emerging elsewhere.[2] Trading on the Beirut stock exchange was suspended in 1983. However, even during the civil war, the liberal bank regulatory system remained largely intact; only a few banks failed, and support from the Lebanese community abroad remained strong.

After the war, structural reforms aimed at modernizing and deepening the financial system, as well as strengthening its soundness, were implemented to lay the ground for Beirut to reemerge as a regional financial center. In the banking system, which to date remains the backbone of the financial sector, consolidation and strengthening of the capital base started, supported by an overhaul and modernization

of the regulatory framework. More recently, regulatory reforms have laid a basis for the development of nonbank financial services, and the Beirut stock market reopened in late 1995.

Structure of the Financial System

Commercial banks remain the most important financial intermediaries despite the significant progress in the development of securities markets in recent years. Besides legal and regulatory factors, the structure of the financial system has also been shaped by the conduct of monetary policy.

Banking System

The structure of the banking system has remained broadly stable during 1990–98. As of mid-1998, there were 71 operating commercial banks, of which 15 were foreign banks, compared with 77 and 12, respectively, at the end of 1990. A total of 7 new banks were chartered during this period, while a number (mostly those severely affected by the war) closed or merged with existing ones, notably during 1990–93 and 1997–98. A law adopted in 1993 and expired in 1998 encouraged consolidation in the banking system, mainly through providing limited concessional loans from the central bank (Banque du Liban(BdL)) for the part of the acquisition cost that is related to the goodwill value.

In mid-1997, a group of about 20 banks accounted for around 80 percent of the sector, measured by the share in deposits, assets, loans, or capital, and for about 90 percent of profits (Table 6.1). The top 8 banks account for about half of the sector. No single bank has a share larger than 10 percent in deposits and 7 percent in loans. This structure has remained broadly constant in recent years. The banking system also includes specialized banks, which may accept only longer-term deposits (exceeding six months' maturity) and must invest a minimum of resources in longer-term loans.[3] The specialized banks

---

[1]See also Saidi (1997) for background on Lebanon's financial sector developments. During the early 1970s services (excluding transport, communication and administration) accounted for about 46 percent of GDP.

[2]Nonresident deposits were equivalent to 20 percent of private resident deposits in the 1970s; by the early 1990s, the ratio had fallen to about half that level.

[3]Defined as loans for which at most 15 percent of principal matures during the first two years of the loan. However, such banks

Table 6.1. Structure of the Banking System[1]
(In percent)

Percentile	1993	1994	1995	1996	1997
Share in assets					
10	51.3	49.6	49.7	49.6	48.6
25	77.4	77.1	78.1	78.2	78.0
50	92.7	92.2	92.4	92.6	92.4
Share in capital account					
10	56.1	55.5	54.7	52.9	52.9
25	79.5	77.1	74.9	77.8	77.9
50	94.1	92	93.6	94.8	94.8
Share in deposits					
10	51.1	50.1	50.6	50.8	50.8
25	80.2	79.5	79.9	79.8	80.0
50	94.0	94.1	93.8	93.9	93.9
Share in loans					
10	49.3	49.2	50.6	48.0	48.0
25	76.2	76.9	78.4	79.1	77.6
50	92.7	93.4	93.2	92.2	92.2
Share in profit and losses					
10	58.5	66.2	57.2	57.2	57.2
25	94.8	82.5	93.8	84.5	87.7
50	100.8	111.4	101.3	103.0	103.0

Source: Banque du Liban.

[1]Percentages in the first column refer to percentiles. For example, in 1993, 25 percent of banks (ranked by size) accounted for 77.4 percent of total bank assets.

comprise mostly semipublic development banks operating in housing, tourism, and industry (see below) and investment bank operations set up by major commercial banks. While the number of specialized banks has doubled from four in 1990 to eight in 1998, such banks remain of marginal importance within the sector.[4] Ownership regulations for specialized banks are the same as for commercial banks.

Ownership Regulations

Foreign banks essentially enjoy national treatment. They are subject, however, to tight constraints

on foreign land ownership (which apply generally for foreign individuals and corporations); they are also expected to invest a minimum of the equivalent of 30 percent of their deposits in Lebanon, and currently the central bank grants license only for one branch in Lebanon. Foreign ownership in banks incorporated in Lebanon must not exceed two-thirds of capital.[5]

Government ownership in the banking industry is limited. The state held a majority in Banque Nationale du Development de l'Industrie et du Tourisme (BNDIT) until 1994, when the bank was restructured and opened for majority, private sector participation. The state also restructured in 1993 the housing bank (Banque de l'Habitat) after it had ceased operations since 1989 owing to losses incurred during the war; state participation is now limited at 20 percent. The bank extends housing loans

---

may lend short-term to other banks and financial institutions, and may invest in short-term treasury bills. Except for lending to the public sector and to "major companies," loans must be collateralized or guaranteed by other banks, and a credit must not exceed 65 percent of the value of the collateral.

[4]Their activity, however, has been rapidly expanding, and total assets of specialized banks were equivalent to 6 percent of commercial banks' assets at the end of December 1997, compared with 2.7 percent at the end of 1994, 3.7 percent at the end of 1995, and 4.5 percent at the end of 1996.

[5]Law 32 of February 11, 1991 stipulates that a third of total shares must be owned by Lebanese natural persons or Lebanese companies held by Lebanese natural persons or joint-stock companies, in which at least a third of shares is held by Lebanese natural persons.

of up to $40,000, either in U.S. dollars or in Lebanese pounds. Social housing is supported by the Institut National de l'Habitat created in 1996 by consolidating similar earlier government-managed schemes; it extends credits for low-income housing at 2 percent and is financed from budgetary resources. A commercial bank (Crédit Libanais), acquired following its collapse by the central bank in the 1980s, was sold to private investors in June 1997.

In the drive to strengthen banks' capital bases, expand shareholding beyond traditional tightly held family ownership, and increase the scope for foreign portfolio investment, banks have been allowed, effective July 1996, to float up to 30 percent of capital on the stock market. Since then, issuance of bank shares has surged. Major banks have recently also mobilized capital abroad through issues of global depository receipts (GDR). The central bank monitors any transfer of nonquoted shares to enforce its ownership regulations and has set limits on the acquisition of shares by the bank's owners and employees.[6]

Prudential Regulations and Bank Supervision

The rebuilding of the financial sector went hand in hand with modernization and strengthening of prudential regulations and banking supervision. International capital adequacy standards, including an 8 percent minimum ratio of capital to risk-weighted assets, were adopted in 1992;[7] banks had to meet these standards by February 1995 but had already met them in 1994. In 1996, the central bank set additional capital requirements in the form of minimum capital levels per head office (LL 10 billion), per domestic branch office (LL 0.25 billion), and per foreign branch office (LL 0.75 billion), but also allowed banks to include real estate holdings valued at market prices in tier 2 capital, provided banks raised an equivalent amount in cash contributing to their tier 1 capital.

Since credits are typically short term and in the form of current account overdrafts, there exist no mechanical rules as to the classification and corre-

sponding provisioning of problem loans.[8] Once supervisors classify loans as doubtful, accrued interest can no longer be accounted for as earning. Provisioning requirements are set by the bank supervisors, based on their evaluation of the extent of the problem and the value of any collateral. Banks need to provide required provisioning immediately, if necessary by using up capital, which then must be reconstituted within one year.

Specific prudential regulations aim at limiting banks' exposure to credit risk, foreign exchange risk, maturity mismatch, and the concentration of borrowers. Net open positions in foreign exchange are limited to 5 percent of capital for the operational and 40 percent for the overall position. Lending to a single borrower is capped at 20 percent of capital, or at 10 percent of equity plus 1 percent of deposits, whichever is less.[9] No rules apply regarding maturity matching in Lebanese pounds assets and liabilities, as the dominant component of the assets (treasury bills and bonds) can be readily refinanced with the central bank. Lending in foreign currency—although it is typically in the form of current account overdrafts and thus has no defined maturity—is capped; the authorities have gradually raised the limit on such lending from 55 percent of foreign exchange deposits in 1991 to 70 percent since May 1997. Banks may issue bonds up to an amount equivalent to six times capital, which in the last two years has helped to secure more long-term funding. Banks may invest in equity up to the equivalent of their capital, but may hold a controlling interest only in companies closely related to the bank's business.

Banking supervision also strengthened in recent years. In 1967, after the collapse of a major bank, parliament separated banking supervision from the central bank and established an independent banking control commission managed by five members appointed by the government. The commission has today about 70 inspectors and its supervisory authority was recently extended to nonbank financial institutions under the new law on fiduciary institutions (June 1996). The commission reports to the governor of the central bank. The High Banking Commission, which includes a senior judge, the director general of the ministry of finance, the chairman of the deposit insurance company, a representative of the Bankers Association, and, as chairmen, the governor and a vice-governor of the central bank, decides on

---

[6]Transfer of shares of more than 5 percent of a bank's total shares requires central bank approval.

[7]The rules underlying the calculation of the ratio of capital to risk-weighted assets (COOKE ratio) are within the ranges recommended by the Basle Capital Accord (July 1988) but tend to be at the low risk end by assigning a zero risk weighting to domestic treasury bills (compared with a 10 percent weighting adopted in some other countries) and a 20 percent risk weighting to foreign currency deposits held with the central bank (compared with up to 50 percent recommended in the Basle Accord), and by including subordinated loans in foreign exchange, on which banks pay interest, in tier 1 capital.

[8]However, the central bank is working together with the Bankers Association on guidelines to promote securitization of credits, which would facilitate the monitoring of credit performance and increase the potential for longer-term lending.

[9]In addition, the total of credit to borrowers, who each account for more than 15 percent of the bank's outstanding credit, must not exceed 800 percent of the bank's capital.

any sanctions against banks failing to meet prudential requirements.

Full on-site inspections for each bank are carried out every second year; more limited on-site inspections for major banks take place up to 10 times a year. Reports are made available also to the bank auditors, who are encouraged to follow up on concerns raised by the bank supervisors. In turn, the control commission also receives the annual audit reports. Off-site, supervisors monitor continuously the operations of banks, based on monthly reports notably on credit-related activities that banks have to submit. By the end of 1997, the adoption of international accounting standards (IAS) became obligatory.

Credit risk management is also supported by the Centrale de Risques established within the central bank in 1962, which is now fully computerized and can respond to requests for information on the creditworthiness of potential clients within 30 days. More recently, the central bank established the Centrale des Impayés, which collects data about defaulters, especially by monitoring and recording check bouncing. Banks are not allowed to extend credit to clients recorded in the Centrale des Impayés.

Deposit Insurance

Following the collapse of a number of banks in the late 1960s, Lebanon established the National Institute for the Guarantee of Deposits (NIGD), which is jointly owned and managed by member banks and the government. It guarantees deposits of small investors (up to LL 1 million between 1988–97 and up to LL 5 million since early 1997) denominated in Lebanese pounds and, until the end of 1998, under a transitory law adopted in 1991, deposits denominated in foreign currency. Banks currently pay an annual premium of 0.05 percent that is matched by equal contributions from the government. The NIGD is allowed to invest accumulated funds in real estate, government papers, and deposits with the central banks. Mostly as a consequence of macroeconomic instability during the civil war, six banks failed during 1989–92. Since at that time the resources of the NIGD had also suffered from the massive inflation, it had to borrow from the central bank to pay about LL 84 billion in insured deposits. The loan was fully repaid by 1994, and there have been no bank failures since.

Payment and Clearing System

The central bank operates a check-clearing system, which was extended to clear checks and payments in foreign currency in recent years after allowing eligible institutions to open foreign currency deposits at the central bank. Faster clearing and settlement, including the use of SWIFT[10] for both international and domestic transactions and the use of magnetized checks have integrated Lebanon's financial system into international payments networks and have reduced counterparty risk (e.g., the recorded number of bounced checks has declined steadily in recent years).

Monetary Policy Instruments

The central bank carries out monetary policy through a number of instruments. Through early 1997, issuance of domestic currency treasury bills and bonds for the sterilization of capital inflows was an important monetary policy instrument. Since then, the issuance of certificates of deposit (with a typical maturity of 40–60 days) and intervention in the foreign exchange market have become more important instruments of monetary policy; the issue of treasury bills for sterilization purposes has been used only occasionally to accumulate foreign exchange reserves. The absence of a deeper secondary market in treasury bills has so far prevented an active use of open market operations (see below). Reserve requirements have not been actively used as an instrument in recent years. Banks must hold the equivalent of 13 percent of Lebanese pound deposits in reserves at the central bank; interest is paid only on 3 percent of these deposits held by banks as special treasury bills. Effective August 1996, reserve requirements were eased as banks were allowed to deduct the equivalent of 13 percent of loans provided for certain productive activities (industry, agriculture, tourism) from obligatory reserves.[11] There are no reserve requirements on foreign currency deposits (although the aforementioned cap on the loan-deposit ratio in foreign exchange effectively enforces substantial precautionary holding of liquid foreign exchange assets). Until March 1997, banks also had to hold treasury bills equivalent to 40 percent of Lebanese pound deposits (this constraint was not binding as banks held treasury bills far in excess of requirements). The central bank stands ready to refinance banks through bilateral repurchase agreements involving treasury bills, but this facility typically has been used only in periods of tension and effectively constitutes the lender-of-last-resort facility.

---

[10]Society for Worldwide Interbank Financial Telecommunications (SWIFT) is a nonprofit, cooperative organization that facilitates the exchange of payment messages between financial institutions around the world.

[11]Such loans also benefit from a 5 percent subsidy paid by the budget.

Securities Markets

Capital markets were underdeveloped at the end of the war but have developed rapidly since then. They are dominated by the primary market for government paper; however, since 1996 the stock market has become active again. Domestic currency treasury bills and bonds are sold through weekly auctions and are the principal instrument for financing the budget. The auctions are conducted by the central bank on behalf of the treasury. Participants in the auctions include banks, other financial institutions, and government bodies, such as the social security fund and the electricity company. Banks may submit unlimited, noncompetitive bids on behalf of the general public and nonresident institutions; these are sold at the weighted average rate of the auction. Until early 1997, all bids at or below the interest rate fixed by the treasury were satisfied; since then, the amount of treasury bills offered has typically been subject to an upper limit given by the financing needs of the treasury. Treasury bills, issued for 3-, 6-, and 12-month maturities, are sold as discount bills while 2-year bonds carry a semiannual coupon. Under an informal understanding with the ministry of finance, the central bank generally refrains from holding treasury bills except in the case of repurchase agreements with commercial banks. Nonresidents have been allowed to purchase treasury bills of any maturity since April 1996, using foreign exchange accounts held with Lebanese institutions (nonresidents are not allowed to hold Lebanese pound deposits).

The secondary market in treasury bills is still rather limited, although the turnover has been rising more recently. There is some trading of treasury bills among banks and between banks and foreign investors, and the central bank operates a market by discounting treasury bills held by individuals. All clearing and settlement of treasury bills in the primary and secondary market occur through the central bank, which is the custodian of all treasury securities.

The Beirut stock exchange (BSE) has been rapidly expanding following its reopening in early September 1995 (trading began in January 1996), but remains still relatively small. The BSE is a public entity, which operates an "official," a "junior," and an over-the-counter (OTC) market (see below). It is also responsible for supervising and regulating the market, and its disciplinary board may impose sanctions on participants not complying with regulations. Privatization of the operational side (to be run by the brokers' association) and establishment of an independent supervisory commission are under consideration. To be listed in the official or junior markets, companies must have a track record of publishing accounts for at least three years, and at least 30 per-

cent of their capital must be tradable and held by at least 50 persons. Small companies may list on the OTC market provided they meet minimum track record requirements. Companies listed are subject to stringent disclosure and transparency requirements and had to adopt international accounting standards before the end of 1998.

As of July 1998, 14 brokers (4 merchant banks and 10 other financial institutions) were accredited to operate on the BSE. Brokers must meet various minimum capital requirements, and their track record is reviewed by international auditing companies as part of the admittance process. Trading is based on a daily fixing session (two fixings for SOLIDERE[12] shares) with the share price set to maximize the number of shares traded. The buying and selling orders are given through the brokers and are not disclosed to the market. Clearing and settlement is carried out by MIDCLEAR, a joint-stock company owned almost entirely by the central bank. Transactions are settled by day T+3. There is no active derivative market, but warrants based on SOLIDERE shares are traded in Luxembourg.

Banks and other financial institutions are free to trade foreign exchange among themselves and with their clients at freely negotiated rates subject to the prudential limits on net open positions. The same holds for exchange houses, which are supervised by the central bank and subject to minimum capital requirements. The central bank intervenes in the market by offering to buy or sell unlimited amounts at a fixed rate, and has thereby effectively set the exchange rate for all transactions in recent years. In early 1997, after gradually widening the bid-ask spread since the fall of 1996, the central bank set a bid-ask spread of LL 10 per U.S. dollar to encourage interbank trading. The central bank does not intervene within the band and does not monitor bilateral transactions between banks. While the central bank is not involved in any forward transactions, commercial banks may take forward positions linked to trade transactions.

Financial Deepening, 1991–97

Soon after the end of the war, the authorities embarked on a program of financial sector reforms that aimed not only at a recovery of the financial system but also at its deepening and development. The overall sectorial policy strategy was based on three key elements: (1) macroeconomic stabilization, (2) strengthening of the regulatory framework for the banking system, and (3) developing the securities markets.

---

[12]A real estate company established in 1994 to manage the reconstruction of central Beirut.

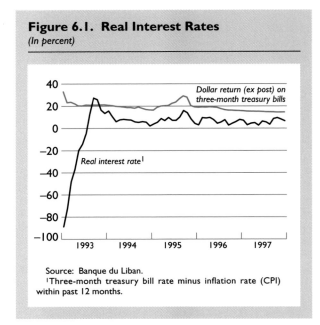

Figure 6.1. Real Interest Rates
(In percent)

Source: Banque du Liban.
[1]Three-month treasury bill rate minus inflation rate (CPI) within past 12 months.

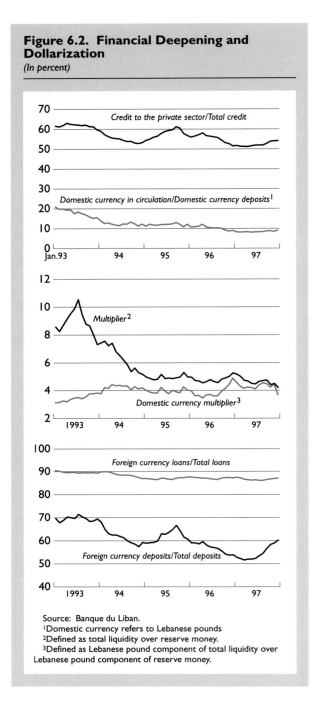

Figure 6.2. Financial Deepening and Dollarization
(In percent)

Source: Banque du Liban.
[1]Domestic currency refers to Lebanese pounds
[2]Defined as total liquidity over reserve money.
[3]Defined as Lebanese pound component of total liquidity over Lebanese pound component of reserve money.

Macroeconomic Stabilization and Financial Deepening

The financial sector was severely affected by the civil war, and its capital was eroded by macroeconomic instability and the sharp depreciation of the Lebanese pound during that period, as banks were not allowed to hold net long foreign exchange positions.[13] Through 1993, the economy remained virtually dollarized, and the income velocity of broader monetary aggregates rose,[14] reflecting highly negative real Lebanese pound interest rates induced by high inflation (Figures 6.1 and 6.2).

However, as stabilization through the exchange-rate-based nominal anchor policy took hold starting in 1993, real interest rates became positive, and dollarization began to decline (relatively rapidly for deposits, much slower for lending to the private sector) (Figure 6.2). While the persistence of dollarization may partly reflect inertia effects (World Bank, 1994), dollarization has also been a traditional phenomenon in Lebanon, as a large part of banks' clients have foreign currency earnings from abroad. The high share of dollar deposits in turn explains partly the predominance of foreign currency lending as transformation into Lebanese pound credits would imply the assumption of additional exchange risk by banks. In addition, Lebanese pound lending

to the private sector was low, as the large financing needs of the government and the high interest rates on treasury bills provided a more attractive outlet for banks' Lebanese pound resources; at the same time, demand for Lebanese pound credit remained weak given the high interest rates charged.

With successful stabilization, financial deepening started, as indicated by a trend-decline in the veloc-

---

[13]For further background on financial deepening during 1991–97, see also World Bank (1994).

[14]Monetary aggregates exclude foreign currency in circulation, for which no reliable data are available.

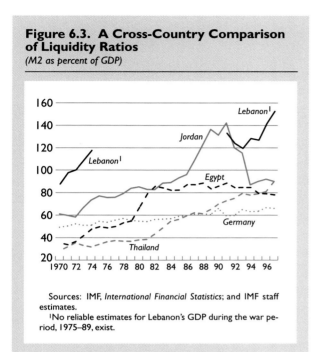

Figure 6.3. A Cross-Country Comparison of Liquidity Ratios
(M2 as percent of GDP)

Sources: IMF, *International Financial Statistics*; and IMF staff estimates.
[1]No reliable estimates for Lebanon's GDP during the war period, 1975–89, exist.

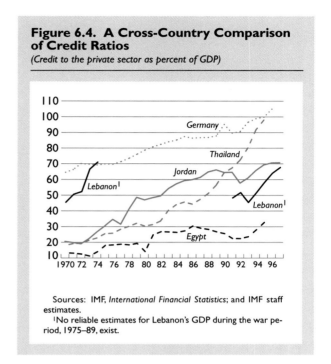

Figure 6.4. A Cross-Country Comparison of Credit Ratios
(Credit to the private sector as percent of GDP)

Sources: IMF, *International Financial Statistics*; and IMF staff estimates.
[1]No reliable estimates for Lebanon's GDP during the war period, 1975–89, exist.

ity of various monetary aggregates, a shift from currency to deposits, and a growing share of private credit as a percent of GDP. A comparison of various indicators of the depth and efficiency of the financial sector in Lebanon[15] and selected other countries points to the relatively high development of Lebanon's banking sector. Financial depth as measured by the ratios of M2/GDP[16] and private credit to GDP seems to have resumed its upward trend of the prewar period, and exceeds the levels of other countries in the region.

At the same time, the lower ratio of M2/GDP in industrial countries and selected high performers points to the underdevelopment of Lebanon's nonbank financial markets, which at more advanced stages of development tend to reduce the importance of monetary instruments (Figures 6.3 and 6.4). The efficiency of Lebanon's banking system, as measured by the ratio of reserve to broad money, also fares well compared with its peers and some Asian

countries and is quite close to the ratios observed in industrial countries (Figure 6.5). Another indicator of the efficiency of financial intermediation may be the relative shares of credit to the private and public sectors. Again, Lebanon compares well with its peers and has a distribution of credit similar to that

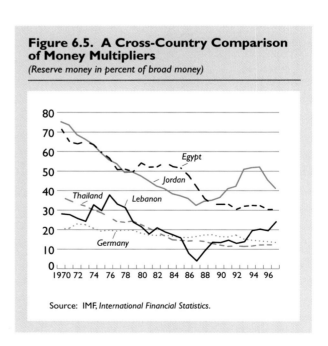

Figure 6.5. A Cross-Country Comparison of Money Multipliers
(Reserve money in percent of broad money)

Source: IMF, *International Financial Statistics*.

---

[15]The indicators discussed in the sequel need, however, to be interpreted with caution owing to two factors: first, foreign currency in circulation, which is probably quite large in Lebanon, is excluded from all monetary aggregates. Second, GDP estimates for the war period are highly unreliable and even the estimates for the 1990s are based on coincident indicators rather than actual accounts.

[16]Even if an estimate for foreign currency in circulation were included in the monetary aggregates, similar trends would be obtained.

Figure 6.6. A Cross-Country Comparison of Private Sector Credit Financing
(Credit to the private sector as percent of total credit)

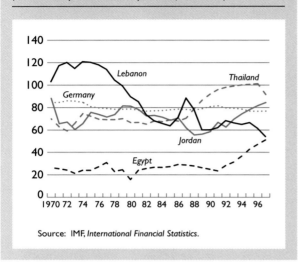

Source: IMF, *International Financial Statistics.*

Figure 6.7. A Cross-Country Comparison of the Share of Commercial Banks in the Banking System
(Commercial bank credit in percent of total credit)

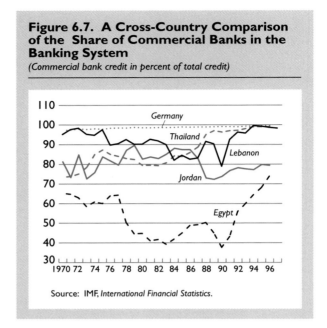

Source: IMF, *International Financial Statistics.*

in industrial countries (Figure 6.6),[17] although the large budget deficits in recent years have begun to increase the share of the public sector. The limited interference of the state in banking is also reflected in the fact that in Lebanon virtually all bank credit is credit from commercial banks, as in industrial countries and some Asian countries (Figure 6.7).

A Sounder Banking System

In addition to greater macroeconomic stability, financial deepening was underpinned by regulatory reforms that aimed at strengthening the soundness of the banking system. At the same time, the legal framework for the development of nonbank financial institutions was put in place, both to enhance competition and to provide functions complementary to the banking system.

Banks quickly became profitable again after the war, as strong demand for credit associated with the rebuilding of the economy and the high rates on government paper kept banking spreads high (Figure 6.8). However, spreads have been on a trend decline in recent years, except in 1995 when they increased owing to domestic political uncertainties. Declining spreads may reflect growing competition within the banking sector, as well as from nonbank financial in-

stitutions and foreign financial markets. Returns on assets are comparable with those of banks in countries belonging to the Organization for Economic Cooperation and Development (OECD), while the average return on equity was very high, in particular

Figure 6.8. Interest Rate Spreads in Banking
(In percent)

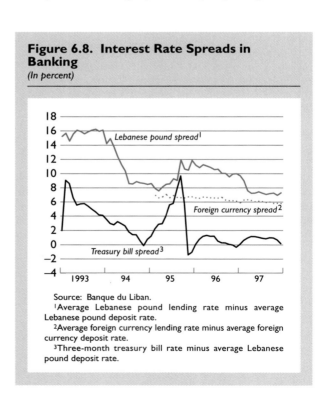

Source: Banque du Liban.
[1]Average Lebanese pound lending rate minus average Lebanese pound deposit rate.
[2]Average foreign currency lending rate minus average foreign currency deposit rate.
[3]Three-month treasury bill rate minus average Lebanese pound deposit rate.

---

[17]Shares of private in total credit of above 100 percent in Figure 6.5 reflect negative credit to the public sector, that is, situations where the public sector on a net basis provides resources to the banking system.

during 1994–95. Healthy returns allowed banks to rebuild their capital base and also strengthen provisioning (Table 6.2). Capital adequacy as measured by the risk-weighted capital adequacy ratio has been steadily improving in recent years, more recently also because regulators have imposed new minimum capital requirements per head office and per branch, on top of the solvency ratio, to be met by the end of 1997. Two smaller banks, accounting together for 0.3 percent of total deposits and 0.4 percent of total credit in June 1997, and which are currently not operating, do not yet meet minimum capital requirements (including a COOKE ratio of 8 percent), and have agreed with the central bank on restructuring

programs to meet the requirements by the end of 1998.

Banks' exposure to various kinds of risk has been contained in recent years (Table 6.2). Exposure to foreign exchange risk, as measured by the difference in assets and liabilities denominated in foreign exchange, has been reduced and since 1993 has been below the prudential limit of 40 percent of capital. Credit risk associated with the foreign exchange risk exposure of borrowers (given the importance of lending in foreign exchange) is difficult to assess but somewhat limited by the fact that most borrowers are, implicitly at least, partially hedged by the dollarization of the economy, even in the nontradables

Table 6.2. Indicators of the Banking System's Financial Strength

	1991	1992	1993	1994	1995	1996	1997
	(In billions of Lebanese pounds)						
Total assets	6,798	14,634	18,809	24,285	29,055	37,183	45,633
Total loans to private sector	1,971	4,804	5,919	7,800	10,320	12,687	15,451
Total capital	148	264	444	676	1,146	1,944	2,990
Portfolio quality							
Problem loans[1]	573	1,297	1,458	1,540	1,621	1,865	2,139
Provisions against problem loans	389	764	809	764	739	773	864
Other provisions for risks and charges	62	122	154	181	204	257	280
	(In percent)						
Problem loans/total loans	29.1	27.0	24.6	19.7	15.7	14.7	13.8
Problem loans/total assets	8.4	8.9	7.8	6.3	5.6	5.0	4.7
Provisions against problem loans/problem loans	10.8	9.4	10.6	11.8	12.6	13.8	13.4
Total provisions/problem loans	78.7	68.3	66.0	61.4	58.1	55.2	53.5
Total capital/problem loans	25.8	20.3	30.5	43.9	70.7	104.2	139.8
Portfolio performance							
Average return on assets	...	...	0.9	1.2	1.1	1.3	1.4
Average return on equity	...	...	38.3	44.4	27.3	25.2	21.7
Capital adequacy							
Total capital/total assets	2.2	1.8	2.4	2.8	3.9	5.2	6.6
Risk-weighted capital adequacy ratio	...	...	...	12.9	16.2	17.0	20.0
	(In billions of Lebanese pounds)						
Exposure to exchange rate risk							
Total foreign currency assets[2]	4,401	9,617	12,476	14,317	17,591	20,503	27,067
Total foreign currency liabilities in foreign exchange[3]	4,458	9,748	12,603	14,466	17,279	19,153	25,916
Net exposure (assets minus liabilities)	−57	−131	−127	−149	312	1,351	1,151
(As percent of capital)	−39	−50	−29	−22	27	69	38
Estimated exposure to real estate market							
Total loans for construction							
(As percent of total loans)	9.5	8.3	9.0	18.9	20.9	21.6	20.6
Foreign currency on-lending ratio (in percent)							
Credits in foreign currency/deposits in foreign currency	...	58.4	47.6	54.2	60.7	63.8	54.7

Sources: Banque du Liban; and IMF staff calculations.

[1]As determined by banking supervision, taking into account credit performance and collateral.

[2]Foreign currency deposits with Banque du Liban, foreign currency loans to private sector, and foreign assets.

[3]Foreign currency deposits of private sector and of nonresidents, liabilities to nonresident banks, subordinated loans and bonds.

Table 6.3. Commercial Banks' Claims on Private Sector Classified by Economic Activity
(End of period)

	1991	1992	1993	1994[1]	1995[1]	1996	1997
	(In billions of Lebanese pounds)						
Agriculture	28	61	75	138	177	206	237
Industry	183	418	530	1,060	1,375	1,703	1,984
Construction	186	398	533	1,447	2,168	2,813	3,285
Trade and services	1,039	2,554	3,165	3,760	4,947	5,907	7,190
Trade	876	2,035	2,544	3,045	3,981	4,635	5,422
Other services	100	321	457	715	966	1,272	1,769
Consumer credit	63	198	164	782	1,130	1,505	2,166
Financial institutions	36	55	50	260	273	432	464
Other	498	1,316	1,541	212	315	442	620
Total	1,971	4,801	5,895	7,660	10,385	13,008	15,947
	(In percent of total)						
Agriculture	1.4	1.3	1.3	1.8	1.7	1.6	1.5
Industry	9.3	8.7	9.0	13.8	13.2	13.1	12.4
Construction	9.5	8.3	9.0	18.9	20.9	21.6	20.6
Trade and services	52.7	53.2	53.7	49.1	47.6	45.4	45.1
Trade	44.5	42.4	43.2	39.7	38.3	35.6	34.0
Other services	5.1	6.7	7.8	9.3	9.3	9.8	11.1
Consumer credit	3.2	4.1	2.8	10.2	10.9	11.6	13.6
Financial institutions	1.8	1.1	0.8	3.4	2.6	3.3	2.9
Other	25.3	27.4	26.1	2.8	3.0	3.4	3.9
	(Percentage change over 12 months)						
Agriculture	...	114.5	23.8	84.1	28.4	16.1	23.9
Industry	...	128.9	26.7	100.1	29.7	23.8	32.7
Construction	...	113.6	34.0	171.2	49.9	29.7	35.1
Trade and services	...	145.8	23.9	18.8	31.6	19.4	29.9
Trade	...	132.3	25.0	19.7	30.8	16.4	20.9
Other services	...	221.9	42.3	56.4	35.0	31.8	68.1
Consumer credit	...	214.1	−17.3	378.0	44.5	33.2	71.2
Financial institutions	...	52.1	−9.2	419.8	4.7	58.3	49.5
Other	...	164.1	17.2	−86.2	48.3	40.2	59.1
Total	...	143.7	22.8	29.9	35.6	25.3	37.3

Source: Banque du Liban.
[1]Revised classification.

sector. Concentration risk remains limited as banks' lending remains diversified among sectors broadly in line with the sectoral composition of GDP. Financing of commercial activity and other services accounted for roughly a stable half of the outstanding stock of credit since 1991 (Table 6.3)[18] and industry for around 13 percent since 1994, while lending to agriculture remained negligible. With reconstruction accelerating in 1994, credit for construction doubled its share in overall credit from the early 1990s. Exposure to the real estate market had thus been rising until the end of 1996, but began declining since. Associated risks, however, appear to be manageable as banks typically financed only around 30 percent of construction or acquisition costs, while the remainder is self-financed. Consumer credit, virtually nonexistent in the early 1990s, also increased its share substantially; an important part seems to be associated with car loans. More generally, the ratio of credit to the private sector to GDP has been rising rapidly, and at about 70 percent indicates a leveraging of the private sector and related vulnerability (Figure 6.4) approaching levels seen in East Asia and in industrial countries. Improved credit-risk management is reflected in a steadily declining share of problem loans in overall loans, which was halved during 1991–97 to 13 percent as problem loans from the war period were

---

[18]The classification of credit by sector was revised in 1994; data before and after that date are not fully comparable.

being absorbed. Furthermore, provisioning against problem loans as well as other risks increased steadily, and total capital has exceeded the total of problem loans since 1996. Finally, maturity mismatch is difficult to measure given that most credits are in the form of callable overdrafts and therefore have, strictly speaking, no maturity. Regarding Lebanese pound components of the balance sheet, while deposits tend to be short term, the large portfolio of treasury bills typically held by banks can be readily refinanced with the central bank should liquidity be needed. As foreign exchange lending is capped as a ratio of foreign exchange deposits, banks hold a large cushion of liquid foreign exchange assets against foreign exchange deposits. Dollarization also carries the risk of rapid shifts between Lebanese pound and dollar deposits; the high liquidity of banks may partly reflect a precautionary position to accommodate such shifts.

Financial Markets

Financial markets have started to play a larger role. The domestic bond market remains dominated by public paper: the stock of domestic currency treasury bills and bonds rose from 49 percent of GDP in 1991 to 86 percent in 1997, as the issuance of these instruments became the main form of domestic budget financing. With improving confidence in financial stability, the share of 24-month bonds in total treasury bills and bonds outstanding increased from 16 percent at the end of 1991 to 54 percent at the end of 1997. Banks remain the dominant holder of treasury bills and bonds, but nonbank holdings increased from a low of 19 percent of the outstanding stock at the end of 1993 to 30 percent at the end of 1997. While this development may reflect to some extent a trend toward disintermediation as observed in other countries, it was enhanced by the banks' slow adjustment of Lebanese pound deposit rates in early 1995, when treasury bill rates surged in response to pressures in the foreign exchange market. Another factor was increased participation of foreign investors in the treasury bill auctions (through local banks or financial institutions) after restrictions on the purchase of short-term bills by nonresidents were lifted in early 1996. The secondary market in treasury bills and bonds remained small, however, partly reflecting the favorable liquidity situation of banks and the short average maturity of outstanding bills. More recently, the secondary market turnover has been rising because of the increased participation of foreign investors and the central bank's practice of rationing competitive bids in the auctions.

The stock market remains dominated by SOLIDERE shares. However, major banks have recently issued shares in the context of their recapitalization

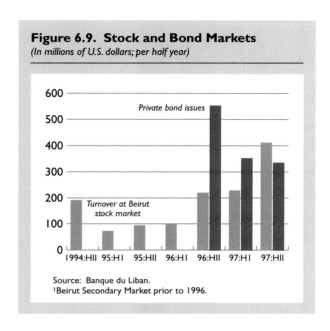

Figure 6.9. Stock and Bond Markets
(In millions of U.S. dollars; per half year)

Source: Banque du Liban.
¹Beirut Secondary Market prior to 1996.

programs, and such issues today account for about a third of shares traded. During the second quarter of 1998, ten companies were listed on the market, including SOLIDERE, three banks, and various cement companies. A number of new listings are planned for the coming years as more companies meet the track record requirements and accounting standards of the exchange. Trading turnover (in terms of U.S. dollars) rose by 30 percent in 1996, and trading in 1997 more than doubled compared with 1996 (Figure 6.9). Market capitalization rose eightfold between June and December 1996, due to the listing of SOLIDERE shares, which were previously traded at a separate institution.

Following the successful launching of sovereign debt on Euromarkets since 1994, private sector bond issues also became more active, both on Euromarkets (Luxembourg) as well as in the local market. In 1996, private banks and a cement company issued bonds for $0.6 billion and another $0.7 billion in 1997. Maturities ranged from 3 to 6 years, and yield spreads over comparable U.S. dollar instruments are about 250–300 basis points; issues traded in local OTC markets commanded higher interest rates. By mid-1998, two Lebanese banks and SOLIDERE had also issued equity through GDR issues for a total of $315 million in London and Luxembourg, and warrants on SOLIDERE shares have been trading in Luxembourg since the end of 1996.

The Challenge for Future Reform

Development of the financial system is a central element of Lebanon's strategy to rebuild its economy for two reasons: first, to mobilize domestic and foreign savings for reconstruction and the further development of the economy, and ensure their efficient allocation; and second, to achieve the authorities' objective of reestablishing Beirut as a regional financial center. While during the 1970s Beirut's traditional role was to channel resources from oil-rich countries to industrial countries, and to serve as a safe haven for regional investors affected by political and economic uncertainties or restrictive policies in their home countries, any future regional role of Beirut would likely be in mobilizing capital and know-how for reconstruction projects and the development of private sector activities (e.g., preparing firms for listing on stock markets) in many countries of the region.

Rapid progress has already been made in strengthening the banking sector. Increased capital requirements have set in motion a consolidation process that will likely result in a system of fewer and stronger banks.[19] Few regulatory or institutional obstacles stand in the way of the development of a modern banking sector, and most of these are currently being addressed: an efficient payment system is being put in place (including electronic transactions, computer-readable checks, and so forth); regulations limiting the share of banks' capital that may be traded publicly are being reviewed; and banks are encouraged to develop securitized forms of credit rather than simple callable overdrafts. Lebanon's openness to foreign competition, including in the banking sector (although somewhat constrained by ownership limitations and limits on the number of branches foreign banks may open) is putting pressure on local banks to raise productivity and lower the cost of financial intermediation.

High and volatile interest rates and the risk of macroeconomic instability contribute to the absence of long-term financing in Lebanese pounds or in foreign currency. Commercial banks remain reluctant to lend longer term, and financing of industrial and other long-gestation projects remains difficult. The authorities have put in place some limited mechanisms directly or indirectly subsidizing longer-term credits and have also increased the scope for banks to raise longer-term resources through equity or bond issues. Specialized banks' lending has been picking up since 1996, apparently largely for housing. However, the development of capital markets will be essential for the mobilization of longer-term financing, which in turn is key for reconstruction and regional finance.

While securities markets are still in their infancy, progress has been made in establishing the legal and institutional framework to encourage their development. In particular, recent legislation has extended the supervisory function of the central bank to finance companies, investment banks, brokers, and other fiduciary institutions, and rules regarding transparency, minimum capital requirements, and other prudential rules have been established. The regulatory framework for the stock market has now been put in place, and the authorities are considering to privatize in the near future the stock market itself, while making the supervisory body fully independent. Clearing and settlement will be further strengthened by draft legislation making MIDCLEAR the sole legal depositary, where securities would be immobilized (eventually a move to full dematerialization is planned). MIDCLEAR already has links to several European and Arab countries allowing settling of transactions between residents and nonresidents; establishment of a regional clearing house modeled after EUROCLEAR (the European securities clearance and settlement system for internationally traded securities) is planned.

Nonetheless, important obstacles need to be overcome to develop the stock market as a major source of capital and an instrument for savers: most Lebanese companies are tightly held by families reluctant to surrender control or submit to more stringent disclosure requirements; international accounting standards have yet to be adopted by most companies; and the absence of market makers limits the liquidity of stocks listed. While capital needs will exert pressure on companies to turn to the stock market, the process will need to be encouraged by enforcing and strengthening accounting and disclosure standards for all incorporated enterprises. Development of the corporate bond market could serve as an intermediate stage for companies in this process. On the demand side, the legal basis for mutual funds will have to be strengthened, further liberalization of restrictions on foreign ownership could boost foreign demand, and over the longer term the development of contractual savings institutions (pension funds, insurance companies, and so forth) would add depth to the market.

Work is ongoing to deepen the secondary market in treasury paper, mainly by strengthening trading between banks (for which the central bank already provides clearing and settlement services) and by developing the framework for banks to resell treasury bills to their clients. However, the short maturity of existing treasury paper and the high liquidity of banks limit the incentives for a more active trading. A gradual move to longer-term government issues in Lebanese pounds would enhance the effectiveness of monetary policy and help establish a longer yield curve, thereby providing benchmarks for pricing private sector issues and increasing the

---

[19]As of late 1997, three merger/acquisitions have taken place.

scope for companies to raise capital through corporate bond issues.

Finally, with continued de-dollarization of the economy, the development of instruments that allow the hedging of foreign exchange risk will gain importance. The authorities are already working on the regulatory framework for a foreign exchange option market.

References

Saidi, Nasser, 1997, "The Reconstruction of Lebanon as a Regional Hub" (unpublished; Beirut: Banque du Liban).

World Bank, 1994, "Lebanon: Financial Policy for Stabilization, Reconstruction and Development," Report No. 13183LE (Washington).

VII Association Agreement Between Lebanon and the European Union

Annalisa Fedelino

Lebanon is negotiating an Association Agreement (referred to hereafter as the agreement) with the European Union (EU). The agreement, which is part of a broader EU initiative in the Mediterranean southern rim (Euro-Med initiative), is expected to cover many dimensions of the economic relationship between the EU and Lebanon, with bilateral trade liberalization in manufactured goods probably being the best known. Other important economic aspects of the planned agreement include the liberalization of services and the right of establishment, the intensification of economic and social cooperation, a comprehensive harmonization of norms, standards, trade-related legislation, and financial and technical support from the EU.

The costs and benefits of the agreement to Lebanon are subject to intense debate. Simulation studies have concluded—similar to studies on other countries involved in the Euro-Med initiative[1]—that costs may outweigh benefits unless preferential trade liberalization is a first step toward broader, nondiscriminatory liberalization, particularly if it fosters greater integration with regional markets. However, costs and benefits of the agreement should be assessed beyond trade creation and trade diversion: dynamic gains can materialize through harmonizing norms and regulations that help promote a more flexible and transparent business environment.

For Lebanon, the agreement has the potential to bring other benefits. The draft agreement under negotiation also provides for the liberalization of services. The service sector has traditionally been Lebanon's main engine of growth, accounting for about two-thirds of domestic production in the prewar years, when Lebanon used to be an important regional center for services, in particular for banking. Many analysts and observers have suggested that services will again be the main force driving economic growth in the future (Saidi, 1996). For this reason, this section tries to offer a broader perspective on how the agreement may help Lebanon to become a regional hub for services, and thus promote economic activity and future growth.

Background to the Association Agreement with Lebanon

The current trade relationship between the EU and Lebanon is regulated by the 1977 agreement and subsequent protocols (Box 7.1). As a result of this agreement and the Generalized System of Preferences (GSP),[2] about 85 percent of all Lebanese exports to the EU benefit from preferential treatment. In return, Lebanon is not required to apply reciprocal or any preferential treatment to EU exports. This asymmetry in treatment is also reflected in different levels of weighted average tariffs: about 3 percent on Lebanese exports to the EU and about 15 percent on EU exports to Lebanon. However, Lebanon's tariffs applied to EU products do not differ from average tariffs applied to products from the rest of the world and are relatively low compared to those prevailing in the region.

Lebanon's trade relations with the EU will be modified by the agreement currently under negotiation. The agreement is part of a broader EU strategy with countries along the southern Mediterranean rim.[3] The strategy, to be implemented through bilateral agreements with participating countries, centers on five main objectives: (1) establishing a free trade area (FTA) for industrial goods between the EU and the participating countries within 12 years; (2) increasing investment flows from the EU; (3) promoting economic links among participating countries;

---

[1]For example, see Galal and Hoekman (1997) and references contained therein.

[2]Under the GSP, the EU unilaterally grants preferential tariff treatment to industrial exports from 146 countries.

[3]These include Algeria, Cyprus, Egypt, Israel, Jordan, Lebanon, Malta, Morocco, the Palestinian Authority, the Syrian Arab Republic, and Tunisia. As of September 1998, agreements were signed with Cyprus, Israel, Jordan, Malta, Morocco, the Palestinian Authority (interim agreement), and Tunisia. Algeria initialed it in May 1997. Turkey has formed a custom union with the EU, which, in addition to the establishment of a free trade area, implies harmonization of all external tariffs.

Box 7.1. Lebanon's Current Trade Regime with the European Union

Lebanon's current trade regime with the European Union is characterized by the following features:

Industrial products. Lebanese industrial exports to the EU receive preferential customs treatment under the Generalized System of Preferences (GSP) and the 1977 trade agreement.

Agricultural products. Exports licences are required for some agricultural products, while for others an agricultural calendar applies. Lebanon does not grant any export subsidy.

Services. The 1977 agreement does not address the issue of trade in services. A number of laws regulates and limits the provision of some services. Most of the restrictions are applied through regulations on the right of establishment.

Nontariff barriers and antidumping. All import quotas in Lebanon were eliminated by the 1995 tariff reforms. Licencing procedures are still applied for some agricultural products and for some materials, part of which are related to the political boycott on Israel. Apart from these measures, the system is nondiscriminatory. A legislative decree of 1967 regulates antidumping measures and countervailing duties, which are very rarely used. These measures are allowed under the 1977 agreement.

Intellectual property rights. Lebanon is a member of the World Intellectual Property Rights Organization, and has signed the most important conventions on intellectual property rights.

Rules of origin. Products made in Lebanon, or of which a sufficiently large share is of Lebanese origin, are eligible for tariff concessions under the 1977 agreement and the subsequent protocols.

(4) improving political and economic dialogue; and (5) channeling EU financial assistance to participating countries, in the form of ECU 4.7 billion in grants from the EU and ECU 4.7 billion in loans from the European Investment Bank (Nsouli, Bisat, Kanaan, 1996).

The latest version of a draft agreement with Lebanon was formulated in March 1998 (Box 7.2). If ratified in the present form, the agreement will change the Lebanese trade regime vis-à-vis the EU mainly in two ways: (1) all tariffs levied on EU products will be reduced to zero over a transition period of 12 years, with no quantitative restrictions; and (2) Lebanese exports to the EU will be exempted from tariffs immediately. Existing restrictions on trade in agricultural products would remain in effect (the current draft agreement does not contain provisions in this regard apart from the fact that negotiations would start five years after its enactment). Moreover, trade between Lebanon and the

EU will benefit from simplified administrative procedures, harmonization of technical standards, and increased cooperation on various fronts. While in all these respects the draft agreement with Lebanon is similar to other Association Agreements with countries in the region, it also foresees a wide-ranging liberalization of trade in services. Other agreements either refer the matter to the adoption of the General Agreement on Trade in Services (GATS) under the World Trade Organization (WTO; e.g., Tunisia and Morocco), or offer a limited commitment to the gradual liberalization of the right of establishment and the supply of services (e.g., Jordan).

Since October 1996, negotiations on the agreement have been suspended upon the Lebanese authorities' request to study further its implications. In March 1997, a Lebanese delegation visited Brussels to advance the negotiations. Progress has stalled on two main issues: the financial envelope and the grace period before the agreement is implemented. The Lebanese authorities feel that the three criteria on which financial assistance is based, namely, population, per capita income, and absorptive capacity (or willingness to undertake reforms), put them at a disadvantage with respect to other countries participating in the Euro-Med initiative; they would prefer the financial assistance to be linked to, among others, the size of the trade deficit. Moreover, they are in favor of a five-year grace period, rather than the standard two years envisaged in some other Association Agreements, to allow the normalization of economic conditions still affected by the consequences of the protracted civil war.

Lebanon is thus now facing the choice between maintaining its economic relations with the EU at their current status or signing a broader new agreement. Given the increasing multilateral liberalization under the auspices of the WTO and the phasing out of the Multifiber Agreement, the value of Lebanon's trade privileges with the EU under the 1977 agreement is likely to decline in the absence of a new agreement.

Main Implications of the Association Agreement: A Review of the Literature

Analyzing the implications of the agreement for Lebanon is not easy. First, the agreements signed so far have not yet been fully implemented, and thus do not allow for the estimation of all costs and benefits associated with the Euro-Med initiative. Second, the empirical analysis of the Lebanese economy is difficult given the data deficiencies in a number of areas. Third, Lebanon's economic structure differs substantially from that of other countries in the region: its economy has been traditionally driven by the pri-

---

Box 7.2. Draft EU Association Agreement with Lebanon

In March 1998, a revised version of the Association Agreement between Lebanon and the European Union was formulated. Below are the main features of the agreement:

Goals of the Agreement

(1) Intensify political dialogue.

(2) Achieve reciprocal free trade in most manufactured goods. Allow preferential access for some agricultural products at a later stage.

(3) Harmonize trade regulations and adopt international technical standards.

(4) Establish conditions for the right of establishment and supply of services.

(5) Increase economic, social, and cultural cooperation.

(6) Secure EU's financial support to help implement these measures.

Trade in Goods

Industrial products. All tariffs on industrial goods will be eliminated over a period of 12 years. According to the current schedule, trade liberalization for many products will start after five years and will be heavily back-loaded.

Textiles and clothing. Lebanon did not participate in the Multifiber Arrangement, and its textile exports to the EU are therefore not subject to restrictions. No specific provisions on textiles are currently in the draft agreement; the annexes to the agreement, to be finalized, will cover specific products, probably including textiles.

Agricultural products. No provision for agricultural products are included in the draft agreement. Article 17 of the draft defers any further measures to liberalize agricultural and fishing products to 2002.

Nontariff barriers, safeguards, and antidumping. No specific provisions are currently in the draft, according to which appropriate implementing rules will have to be adopted within five years after the agreement becomes effective.

Trade in Services

According to Article 31, Lebanon and the EU both commit to grant most-favored-nation (MFN) treatment to all services covered by the GATS. Exceptions are made for air transport, inland waterways, and maritime transports, where the principle of unrestricted access to the international market and traffic on a commercial basis are applied (Article 32). To this end, all unilateral measures and obstacles that might constitute disguised restrictions and have discriminatory effects on the free supply of international maritime transport will be abolished.

Right of Establishment

According to the draft Association Agreement, freedom of establishment would become immediately effective. EU companies will receive national treatment in Lebanon, and Lebanese companies will enjoy MFN treatment in the EU.

Intellectual Property Rights

Various agreements on intellectual property rights will have to be signed within three years after the enactment of the Agreement becomes effective.

Rules of Origin

There are no provisions for the cumulation of rules of origin. Only goods largely of Lebanese origin would qualify.

Legal Framework

The draft Agreement calls for the harmonization of laws, such as competition and antitrust legislation.

---

vate sector and has enjoyed a liberal economic regime, including a relatively nonprotectionist trade policy. Thus, the agreement may affect Lebanon's economy differently, and parallels with the experiences of other countries in the region cannot be easily drawn.

Most recent papers on the agreement with Lebanon have focused on three main issues: (1) the welfare implications of the agreement through its effect on trade creation and trade diversion; (2) the fiscal implications associated with the establishment of a free trade area, and the related loss of customs revenues; and (3) the competitiveness implications for the domestic industries of the changes in the effective rates of protection. There are also other relevant issues, such as the dynamic gains related to the im-

provement and harmonization of the regulatory environment. While difficult to quantify because of their lack of a price equivalent, these factors play an important role in promoting a business environment that can attract domestic and foreign investment, and, therefore, enhance growth prospects.

Welfare Implications of the Agreement

Following the establishment of a free trade area between the EU and Lebanon, trade between them is likely to increase (trade creation), but possibly at the expense of trade with the rest of the world (trade diversion). How these factors would affect Lebanon's welfare depends on the characteristics of its import and export markets.

Table 7.1. Composition of Imports by Source, 1996

	Imports (As percent of total)	Origin	
		EU (As percent of category)	Other
Transport equipment	17.80	49.6	50.4
Machinery and equipment	16.90	57.7	42.3
Other heavy manufactures	16.30	42.4	57.6
Chemicals	10.60	65.7	34.3
Processed food	8.00	34.2	65.8
Petroleum and coal products	6.50	42.8	57.2
Light manufactures	5.00	51.8	48.2
Livestock	4.90	58.8	41.2
Agricultural products, nongrains	3.70	15.6	84.4
Textiles	3.50	41.1	58.9
Apparel	2.70	55.1	44.9
Agricultural products, grains	2.20	4.4	95.6
Natural resources	1.80	56.0	44.0

Sources: Martin (1996); and IMF staff calculations.

Lebanon's Import Market

The EU represents by far Lebanon's most important source of imports, accounting for about 50 percent of total imports in 1996.[4] The United States is another important trade partner (11 percent of total imports), while other countries of the Middle East and North Africa (MENA) account for only 8 percent. Owing to the elimination of tariffs, the agreement has the potential to make the EU an even more dominant import partner for Lebanon in volume terms. The composition of imports by source provides useful information regarding the market shares of EU imports in specific product categories. Table 7.1 shows that, with the exception of grain and nongrain products, imports in 1996 were almost evenly distributed between the EU and the rest of the world. This even distribution does not seem to suggest prima facie that the implementation of the agreement may affect some import categories more than others.

As tariffs on imports from the EU are gradually eliminated, imports from non-EU countries could suffer from trade diversion, depending on the relative magnitude of the tariffs, the price elasticities, and the elasticity of substitution between suppliers. Data on weighted average tariffs (Table 7.2) indicate that EU and non-EU imports were burdened in 1995 with about the same degree of tariff protection (about 15 percent). Thus, the future elimination of tariffs on EU products could give these products a significant advantage.

---

[4]This compares with 45 percent for Egypt, 44 percent for Turkey, 70 percent for Tunisia, and 65 percent for Morocco.

Lebanon's Export Market

Exports by origin present a different picture than imports. While the EU accounts for only 17 percent of total exports, countries in the region receive a large share of Lebanese exports: about 17 percent by countries participating in the Euro-Med initiative and 37 percent by other Arab countries. Given the small share of Lebanese exports destined for the EU and the low EU tariff rates currently applied to Lebanese products, it seems that Lebanon would benefit only marginally from the elimination of EU tariffs. On the other hand, regional countries import comparatively more Lebanese products, and they subject Lebanese exports to much higher protection than those of industrial countries, as indicated by average and weighted tariff rates (Table 7.3). For this reason, Lebanese exports could greatly benefit from reciprocal trade liberalization with these countries.

Assessing the Welfare Effects

On the import side, the elimination of tariffs will affect welfare through lowering import prices on EU goods. Consumers will be better off through an increase in their welfare, while some producers will be worse off because they will not be able to withstand the increased competition (see below). This would trigger shifts in the factor allocation from import-substituting to export-oriented industries and would enhance the allocative efficiency according to the principle of comparative advantage. On the export side, the welfare effects could be small since Lebanon already enjoys free access to the EU mar-

Table 7.2. Weighted Average Tariff Rates and Import Shares, 1995

(In percent)

	Weighted Average Tariff Rates	Import Shares
European Union	15.1	53.6
Syrian Arab Republic	58.7	8.5
Tunisia	24.3	0.1
Japan	16.1	3.9
Jordan	15.0	0.6
United States	14.8	10.6
Egypt	14.1	0.9
Morocco	12.0	1.1
Total	15.4	100.0

Source: Martin (1996); and IMF staff estimates.

Table 7.3. Protection Against Lebanese Exports, 1995

	Tariff Rates	
	Simple average	Weighted average
European Union	4.6	3.9
United States	4.5	2.8
Japan	4.6	2.8
Egypt	42.2	31.0
Tunisia	33.2	24.8
Jordan	28.4	22.0
Algeria	22.9	16.4
Morocco	22.8	19.0
Syrian Arab Republic	11.0	12.6

Source: Martin (1996).

ket for most industrial goods, although its exports are subject to some rules of origin that could be changed in the context of the agreement; however, to the extent that export producers use as input cheaper imports, their competitiveness might be enhanced.

Martin (1996) quantifies the welfare effects of the agreement in a computable general equilibrium model. Table 7.4 summarizes the main results of this simulation study on the expected change in percent of four main variables with respect to the baseline year (1996): (1) imports (from the EU and total import volume); (2) exports (to the EU and total export volume); (3) nontraded good prices (as an indication of real exchange rate developments); and (4) real expenditure.[5]

The first column shows the impact of the implementation of the agreement. While substantial trade is created with the EU (imports from the EU increase by 23 percent), trade is also diverted away from the rest of the world: as a result, the total import volume increases by a paltry 0.5 percent. Lower import prices reduce prices of nontradables and the incentives to substitute away from domestic goods to cheaper imports. The reduction of tariffs make exports more profitable, as shown in the increase in exports both to the EU and to the whole world. Overall, the agreement results in a small welfare loss of 0.3 percent with respect to base-period expenditure, as trade diversion costs outweigh trade-creation benefits.

In the second column, it is assumed that, in addition to the agreement, trade is liberalized with all the

other countries in the region. Imports from the EU grow less than in the previous scenario and there is no trade diversion (total imports grow by 3.4 percent). A larger (and less preferential) trade liberalization boosts exports, both to the EU and the world in general. Free trade gives rise to positive welfare gains (0.6 percent).

Should Lebanon decide not to join the agreement and continue to benefit from most-favored-nation (MFN) treatment by the EU, the outcome would be as shown in the third column. While the EU would eliminate its tariffs on imports from other countries, Lebanese exports to the EU would still benefit from MFN treatment. This has a positive impact on Lebanon's exports to the EU, which increase by 11 percent. The impact on total exports is insignificant (total export volume increases by only 0.2 percent), however, as exports to the EU represent a limited share of total exports. In this scenario, very small welfare gains are generated (real expenditure increases by 0.1 percent).

The results in Table 7.4 depend on a number of assumptions, including (1) the elasticity of substitution among competing suppliers (the higher, the larger trade diversion), (2) the starting net trade position (given the assumption of unchanged trade balance), and (3) the liberalization of nontariff barriers along with tariffs. The simulation of alternative scenarios that are based on different assumptions for these key parameters shows that the implementation of the agreement accompanied by trade liberalization with other countries in the region (because of larger gains from reciprocal liberalization with countries that represent large export markets) remains the trade policy strategy with the most favorable welfare implications.

---

[5]Martin's analysis is broader than reported here; the spirit of the results is nonetheless the same.

Table 7.4. Some Effects of Trade Liberalization
(Change in percent with respect to baseline)

	Association Agreement	Association Agreement Plus Trade Liberalization with Other Associated Countries[1]	Status Quo
Imports from the EU (volume)	23.4	13.3	0.2
Total import (volume)	0.5	3.4	0.2
Exports to the EU (volume)	8.5	17.0	11.1
Total export (volume)	8.5	15.8	0.2
Nontraded goods price	−5.9	−7.2	0.2
Real expenditure	−0.3	0.6	0.1

Source: Martin (1996).

[1]The associated countries include Algeria, Cyprus., Egypt, Israel, Jordan, Lebanon, Malta, Morocco, the Palestinian Authority, the Syrian Arab Republic, and Tunisia.

Fiscal Implications of the Agreement

One of the most important effects of establishing a free trade area is the loss of tariff revenue. In Lebanon, this loss will be relatively large because of the large share of customs duties and other taxes on imports in tax revenue (almost 60 percent in 1996).

According to the draft agreement, the tariff reduction, covering a period of 12 years, will be heavily back-loaded.[6] Two years after the agreement becomes effective, the 2 percent tariff rate will be reduced to zero. Starting from year 6 onward, all other tariffs will be progressively lowered according to the reduction factors shown in Table 7.5. By year 13, all tariffs will be equal to zero.

---

[6]Lebanon's tariff schedule includes the following rates: 2, 5, 10, 15, 20, 25, 30, 35, 40, 50, 80, and 100 percent. In 1996, the 10 percent and 30 percent rates each generated more than 15 percent of total customs revenues; about 60 percent of total customs revenues were accounted for by the 0–30 rates. The last three rates are not widely used and generate insignificant revenues.

According to this schedule, Abdel-Rahman and others (1997) estimate that the revenue loss would initially be small at about 0.2 percent of GDP in year 3 but would then increase progressively to 4.2 percent of GDP by year 13 (with a steep acceleration in the last three years: 2.6 percent of GDP in year 11 and 3.4 percent of GDP in year 12). These results are based on a static analysis, assuming that imports originating from the EU and their shares over GDP will remain constant over the transition period. Possible changes in the import composition are not factored into this analysis. Dynamic calculations that take into account indirect effects through trade diversion imply that revenue losses would still be in the range of 3–4 percent of GDP, since positive income effects related to reduced prices would probably benefit imports from both the EU and the rest of the world (Helbling, 1996).

Diwan (1997) considers whether increased financial assistance from the EU could help compensate for forgone revenue. He argues that, since the EU's

Table 7.5. Reduction Factor for Tariff Rates During the Transition Period of the Association Agreement

	Year							
	6	7	8	9	10	11	12	13
Reduction factor	0.92	0.84	0.76	0.68	0.54	0.40	0.20	0.00

Table 7.6. Average Effective Rates of Protection

	Effective	After 3 years	After 6 years	After 9 years	After 12 years
Mean	0.22	0.16	0.14	0.11	0.05
Standard deviation	0.21	0.16	0.14	0.11	0.05

Source: Hoekman (1996).

contribution to future Lebanese financing is not expected to exceed 2 percent of GDP, half of which would be in the form of loans (implying higher servicing costs to be financed by higher revenue), the loss of revenue will only be partially offset.

Changes in Effective Rates of Protection and Implications for Competitiveness of Domestic Industries

While Lebanon's nominal tariff rates rank among the lowest in the region, Lebanese industries nevertheless enjoy quite high effective rates of protection (ERPs),[7] averaging 22 percent (Hoekman, 1996).[8] In general, the ERPs vary substantially between different products (the standard deviation is 22 percentage points), ranging from a low of zero for grain to about 60 percent for apparel and 84 percent for transportation equipment. These ERPs still compare favorably with those prevailing in neighboring countries, for example, Jordan, with an average ERP of about 50 percent, and Egypt, with an average ERP of about 70 percent.

With the gradual tariff reduction required by the agreement, ERPs will decline. The back-loaded, tariff-reduction scheme described above will have very little impact on the ERPs during the first five years, thereby allowing Lebanese industries to adjust over a longer time (Table 7.6). However, during the last three years of the transition, when about one-half of the tariff reduction materializes, the average ERP will be drastically reduced, by as much as 70 percent by year 12.

The pressures for domestic industries to adjust will be partially offset by other factors. As reconstruction nears completion, prices of nontradables are likely to decrease, as a result of increased efficiency of the business environment, improved services, upgraded infrastructure, and removal of "bottlenecks." These factors will increase the competitiveness of the Lebanese economy, thus reducing the impact of increased external competition under the FTA and partly compensating for the reduction in the ERPs. In particular, the higher the share of services in inputs, the larger the degree that the supply of better services can improve the competitiveness of a product. Hoekman (1996) estimates that, assuming that costs of services in Lebanon decline linearly by 10 percent over the agreement implementation period and that the prices of services remain constant, the average ERP will increase from 4 percent to 10 percent. The importance of services in making an economy more competitive is further explored below.

Dynamic Gains from Harmonizing Regulatory Regimes

The agreement with the EU changes more than just the border barriers to trade: it implies deeper integration in terms of policies and regulatory regimes. Hence, the gains and losses from the agreement have to be evaluated beyond the narrow focus on trade creation and diversion; important dynamic gains can materialize from harmonizing rules and regulations.

Such harmonization will improve Lebanon's business environment by establishing a level playing field through clear and transparent rules, which will help attract foreign direct investment (FDI). This last aspect is particularly relevant to Lebanon, given its recent history of war and its need to attract sustainable capital flows to help rebuild the country. Anchoring reforms and policies to a credible "policy anchor" will contribute to reducing uncertainty and enhancing confidence in its modernization and stabilization efforts. The deeper policy coordination and collaboration between Lebanon and the EU envisaged by the draft agreement will result in removing administrative bottlenecks and reducing transaction costs and uncertainty, which may currently hinder investment decisions of Lebanese and foreign eco-

[7]The ERP is equal to $(V_d - V_w) / V_w$, where V_d is the domestic value added per unit of a good at domestic prices (including tariffs), and V_w is the value added per unit of a good at world prices under zero tariffs.

[8]The calculation of ERPs requires input-output data that are not yet available for Lebanon. Hoekman (1996) applies input-output data for Egypt, Jordan, and Tunisia in his calculations. In all three cases, results are quite similar.

Box 7.3. Protection of Services in Lebanon

Services are protected by limiting or restricting market access or national treatment through general regulations and sector-specific regulations.

General Regulations

Foreign labor. Foreigners intending to work in Lebanon need a work permit from the ministry of labor. Applications must be submitted through a Lebanese employer. They also need a residency permit from the relevant authorities. Working permits are valid for two years and are renewable. Any change in occupation requires approval from the ministry of labor. Some professions are restricted to Lebanese. As employees, foreigners cannot work as managers or assistant managers of local banks, salespersons, exchange officers, lab technicians, goldsmiths, pharmacists, electricians, doorpersons, guards, school teachers (except for foreign languages), engineers, barbers, drivers, or waiters. As employers, foreigners cannot be involved in construction, jewelry trading, shoe manufacturing, furniture making, confectionery, printing, publishing, and cannot work as a barber or mechanic.

Acquisition of land. Foreigners are not allowed to acquire real property in Lebanon exceeding 10,000 square meters for the activities of their companies, unless the majority of shares belongs to Lebanese individuals or companies (for general partnership or limited liability companies) or if at least one-third of the shares is owned, subscribed, and registered by Lebanese shareholders (for limited partnership companies or stock companies).

Operations of companies. All companies are required to register with the Commercial Register of the Tribunal of the district where the commercial activities are exercised. Certain activities are restricted (see above).

Source: *Guide for Investors in Lebanon* (1997).

Joint-stock companies can be fully or majority foreign owned and controlled. However, the majority of the members of the board of directors have to be Lebanese citizens.

Provision of Public Services. If a company provides a public service, at least one-third of the company's capital has to be owned by Lebanese shareholders. There are no general regulations defining a public service; sectoral regulations list some of these activities.

Specific Regulations

Banking and financial institutions. The establishment of any type of financial institution is subject to a special license from the Banque du Liban, which has discretionary power to approve or reject the licence. Foreign ownership of banks incorporated in Lebanon cannot exceed two-thirds of the capital. Moreover, foreign banks cannot open more than one branch in each of Lebanon's five districts. Reciprocity is applied (de facto) in granting licences to foreigners.

Insurance services. Currently, the insurance sector is dominated by foreign companies. Crossborder trade in insurance is limited. Insurance cannot be taken with companies not registered in Lebanon, the only exception being the transport insurance of imported goods.

Tourism. Apart from the work limitations described above, permits from the ministry of tourism are required to establish tourism-related activity (hotels, restaurants, and so forth). Permits can be granted to foreigners.

Legal services. The provision of legal services is subject to reciprocity. Foreign lawyers can operate if they have certification from one of the two bar associations in Lebanon. A foreign legal firm can operate only through a Lebanese firm.

Maritime transport. There is no cargo reservation law. However, Lebanese ships have preferential treatment when docking in Lebanese ports, and they benefit from lower charges and taxes than foreign vessels.

---

nomic agents. By fostering foreign and domestic investment, the harmonization of rules can be important in promoting growth.

Liberalization of Trade in Services

Protection of services takes on different forms compared with the protection of goods. Protection of services usually targets producers, not products, for two main reasons: (1) services are invisible, so the usual means of protection applied at the border, such as tariffs, are ineffective, and (2) since the delivery of services requires in most cases a presence in the importing market, service protection requires barriers to foreign establishment in a domestic market, for example, through restrictions on investment, rather than tariff or border barriers. This also implies that the liberalization of services involves the liberalization of the right of establishment, especially for those services that are nonstorable and have to be consumed at the location where they are produced.

The main measures limiting or restricting market access in the service sector in Lebanon are described in Box 7.3. In summary, the right of establishment is already quite liberal, especially when compared with other countries in the region. Working permits and licenses are required for certain activities; limits to non-Arab ownership of land are in place; and companies providing services of public interest are required to have at least one-third Lebanese ownership.

Since the protection of services is not based on tariffs and thus does not have a price equivalent, it is difficult to evaluate the costs of protecting services, and thus the benefits of their liberalization. No comprehensive theoretical and empirical studies exist on the welfare implications of the liberalization of services;[9] limited results exist for specific sectors.[10]

Service liberalization can take place at two levels: the product level or the factor level. For example, in international banking, the service factor is a composite factor of managerial and technological skills, while the service product is the set of services that a bank can provide to its customers. The liberalization of the market for banking factors would require banks to be granted the right to establish, for example, to open branches in a foreign country, while the liberalization of the market for banking products would allow residents of a country to acquire banking services from foreign banks (e.g., by opening accounts abroad and managing transactions through them).

If Lebanon is considering liberalizing trade in services, the question arises whether trade in service factors or service products should be liberalized and what would be the gains in each case. With the liberalization of the markets for service factor inputs, Lebanon would allow foreign institutions the right to establish and operate under the same conditions as the domestic ones (through FDI, privatization, deregulation); with the liberalization of the markets for service products, Lebanon would allow foreign institutions the right to do business with domestic residents.

The implications of these options can be illustrated with the help of a simple specific-factor model developed by Jones and Raune (1990) and extended to the case of Lebanon (see the appendix). The model is based on a number of simplifying assumptions, such as (1) the world is composed of only two countries, Lebanon and the EU; (2) these two countries produce only two goods, one manufacturing product, M, and one service product, S (for simplicity, one can think of the manufacturing product as a generic product that comprises overall production

except services, S); and (3) each product is produced with the combined use of a specific factor (used only in the process of that good) and labor. The model also assumes that Lebanon possesses a relative comparative advantage in producing the service product over the manufacturing product even though the EU may have an absolute advantage in producing both M and S. Based on these and other assumptions described in the appendix, the model shows that Lebanon would always gain from liberalizing trade in services, irrespective of whether the liberalization applies to the market for the service factor input or the market for the service products. The size of the welfare gains from the liberalization of the right to establish or the right to do business, however, would depend on Lebanon's initial conditions (i.e., its endowment the service specific factor input, its remuneration, and the price of the service product, which, before the liberalization, is determined by supply and demand conditions in the Lebanese market) as compared with the EU's initial conditions.

The analysis in the appendix shows that, based on the assumption that the service-specific factor input is relatively scarce in Lebanon (so that its remuneration there is higher than in the EU), gains from the agreement with the EU are maximized if the service factor is liberalized. This is consistent with the fact that the liberalization of the right of establishment will help attract FDI and thus improve the human capital and technology available to Lebanon.

The assumption about the relative scarcity of the service factor inputs in Lebanon is obviously critical to derive the above results. However, the result that benefits are to be reaped from service liberalization is robust and can be extended to other cases. For example, if Lebanon is assumed to have a relative abundance of the service factor compared with the other countries in the region, then its gains would be maximized from the liberalization of the service products (see the appendix).

In summary, if Lebanon is assumed to experience a relative scarce supply of the service factor input vis-à-vis another trading partner (implying that the service factor input has a higher remuneration in Lebanon), then it would maximize its welfare gains from liberalizing the right of establishment in its trade relations with such a country. In the simplified framework of this paper, this could be the case with the EU. Alternatively, if Lebanon is assumed to have a relative abundance of the service factor input vis-à-vis another trading partner (where the remuneration of this factor is higher than in Lebanon), then the liberalization of the right to do business or of the market for services in the partner country would maximize Lebanon's welfare gains. This could be the case, for example, with other countries in the region. In both cases, and whichever form of liberal-

---

[9]Brown and others (1995) claim that the welfare gains from reducing industrial tariffs under the Uruguay Round could have been three times higher if the services barriers had been lowered by 25 percent.

[10]For example, in the United States the Jones Act does not allow foreign shipping firms to transport goods or people from one U.S. location to another (for the reason of maintaining an adequate domestic marine capacity to meet defense needs). It is estimated that the welfare costs of protecting shipping services is in the range of $3 billion a year (Hoekman and Braga, 1997).

ization is pursued, Lebanon would benefit from the liberalization of markets for services. Furthermore, the model also shows that opening up trade would not hurt labor (assumed to be immobile), since real wages would rise as a result of the decline in the price of the service products that follow the trade liberalization.

Conclusions

This section has reviewed the main results of the literature on the Association Agreement between Lebanon and the EU and offered some considerations on the liberalization of services envisaged under the draft agreement. Three main conclusions emerge. First, while the adjustment costs and losses are likely to materialize early in the implementation period, the benefits will unfold over a longer time horizon. Whether benefits will offset or even exceed the losses depends on a number of factors. In particular, the Euro-Med initiative will be beneficial for Lebanon and the other Arab countries involved if accompanied by increased deregulation and liberalization within the region. The envisaged Arab Free Trade Area may represent an important first step in this direction.

Second, the agreement with the EU can provide Lebanon with an important "policy anchor" that could bolster the credibility of Lebanon's reform efforts. In this respect, the harmonization of rules and regulations will increase the transparency and efficiency of Lebanon's business environment, a prerequisite for mobilizing domestic and foreign investment.

Third, the agreement offers Lebanon an important opportunity to liberalize its service sector, allowing it to reap significant benefits. Liberalization of services may be more effective in the diffusion of technological progress than liberalization of trade in goods to the extent that it involves movement of factors of production rather than of products. Since foreign direct investment is the major mode of delivery for services across countries, liberalizion can be useful in attracting more of it to Lebanon, and thus act as an important factor in promoting growth. This is also essential if Lebanon wants to regain its position as a service hub for the region.

Appendix. A Specific-Factor Model for Liberalization of Services

This appendix illustrates how Lebanon can benefit from liberalizing its service sector. Results are based on an extension of the simple specific-factor model developed by Jones and Ruane (1990) to the case of

Lebanon. The model assumes a world with two countries, Lebanon (L) and the EU (an asterisk denotes variables referring to the EU, which is considered the foreign country). Lebanon produces two goods, one manufacturing product, M, and one service product, S (for simplicity, one can think of the manufacturing product as a generic product that comprises overall production except services, S). Each product is produced with the combined use of a specific factor (used only in the process of that good) and labor, N. That is, the manufacturing product is produced using K_M and N while the service product S is produced using K_S and N. Labor is assumed to be immobile across countries, while every specific factor in nonservice activity is internationally mobile. The model allows for (1) competition and free trade in all nonservice products (M and M^*), and (2) different technology in the two countries. The model also assumes that the EU may have an absolute advantage in producing both M and S but that Lebanon possesses a relative comparative advantage in producing the services product.

In the model, the following conditions hold:

- The price of manufacturing goods and the return to factors of production are determined in the world market; for simplicity and without loss of generality, it is assumed that EU prices are in line with world prices.
- The wage rate in Lebanon differs from the wage rate in the EU, for Lebanon's technology is assumed to differ from that used in the EU.[11]
- In Lebanon, the specific factor used in the service sector and the service product have their return and price determined by domestic demand and supply conditions (since both markets are protected in Lebanon and thus are closed to international competition).

This last condition is described in the right-hand panel of Figure 7.1, showing the demand and supply for the service product in Lebanon. The left-hand panel of Figure 7.1 describes the relationship between Lebanon's return to the service factor, r_s, and Lebanon's price of the service product, p_s. The technology and the skills of factors are assumed to differ in Lebanon from the EU, whose price and remuneration of services are p_s^* and r_s^*. The figure is designed so that Lebanon is endowed with relative small amounts of the service factor: the supply curve X_s intersects the demand curve D_s at a point such as

---

[11]Competitive conditions ensure that

$$w = \frac{p_m^* - a_{Km} r_m^*}{a_{Nm}},$$

where w is the wage rate, p_m^* and r_m^* are the world product price and the return to the specific factor in the manufacturing sector, respectively; a_{Km} and a_{Nm} are the capital and labor input-output coefficients in the manufacturing sector.

F', implying a high autarky service product and service prices (given by F on the left-hand side) relative to the one prevailing in the EU. Moreover, the remuneration of the service factor in Lebanon exceeds that in the EU as r_s is larger than r_s^*.

What will be the impact for Lebanon of liberalizing its services with the EU? The answer depends on how it decides to liberalize, whether at the product or at the factor level. Suppose first that Lebanon considers the option of liberalizing trade in the service product. From the initial point F', free trade in the service product would lead to an output contraction along the supply curve given by $x_s(K_s)$ and an amount GE' would be imported at the relatively lower EU (world) price p_s^*. Despite the lower domestic output, the lower relative price raises real income. Letting X_s denote the level of imports, the gains from such a trade are given by:

$$\Delta W = \int_0^{\bar{X}_s} [p_s^* - p_s^F(x_s)] \, dX_s. \tag{1}$$

Suppose now that Lebanon allows free trade in the service factor with the EU. This would allow the EU service factors to enter Lebanon's service market with the service product remaining nontraded. The inflow of the foreign specific factor K_s^* shifts the supply curve rightward until the local price p_s is achieved. Service factors flow into Lebanon until the domestic return to the service factor is equated with the world return, r_s^*. In this case, the gains for Lebanon from opening trade in the service factor are given by:

$$\Delta W = \int_0^{K_s^*} [r_s(p_s(K_s^*)) - r_s^*)] \, dK_s. \tag{2}$$

In both cases, the model supports the argument that Lebanon gains from opening the service sector to trade. Additionally, it suggests that given Lebanon's initial conditions relative to the EU, trade in the service factors (right to establish) is preferable to trade in the service products (right to do business). One can see this by comparing area $GF'E'$ to area $AF'B'$ in Figure 7.1.

The initial assumption pertaining to Lebanon's relative scarcity of the service factor is obviously critical for the result derived above. However, the general result that Lebanon gains from liberalizing its services trade is robust; the model can easily be extended to cover different cases. Consider, for example, the case where Lebanon has a comparative advantage in services and an abundance of the service factor.[12] In this case, opening up trade in the service factor will lead

---

[12]Such a composition of endowments would imply that the position of the supply curve in the right-hand panel of Figure 7.1 is located outward relative to the existing one. The autarky point could be at a point like M in the left-hand panel.

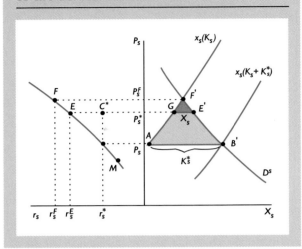

Figure 7.1. Supply and Demand for Service Products, Their Prices, and Remuneration to the Service Factor

to an outflow of the service factor and will shift the domestic supply curve inward. Output of the service product will fall, however, as the service factor will earn more abroad than it was earning at home, and real incomes in Lebanon will increase. If, instead, Lebanon opens up its trade to service products, its technological advantage in producing the service product coupled with its abundance of the service factor would result in a significant expansion of the service sector and the production of S. It is straightforward to show that in this case trade in service products (right to do business) is preferable to trade in service factors (right to establish).

In summary, if Lebanon's endowment with the service factor is scarce relative to that of a trading partner (and thus the service factor has a higher remuneration in Lebanon), then Lebanon would maximize its welfare gains from liberalizing the market for the service factor in its trade relations. For example, this could be the case with the EU, where Lebanon would benefit more from the liberalization of the service factor rather than the service product. Alternatively, if Lebanon has an abundance of the service factor relative to a trading partner (where the remuneration of this factor is higher than in Lebanon), then the liberalization of the service product market in the partner country maximizes Lebanon's welfare gains. This could be the case with the countries in the region. In either case, the price of the service product would be the international price p_s^*.

Returning back to the example described in Figure 7.1, we can examine the impact from Lebanon's de-

Figure 7.2. Prices of Service Products and Remuneration to Service Factors

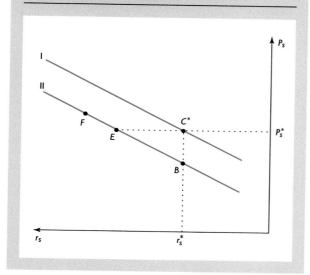

ever, depends on the initial conditions with respect to the trading partner before the liberalization takes place. Furthermore, opening up trade does not have to hurt the immobile factor, that is, labor, as the real wage will rise, especially as the price of the service product will fall following the trade liberalization.

References

Abdel-Rahman A.M., Thomas Helbling, Andersen Erik, and Percy Kierstead, 1997, "Lebanon: The Association with the European Union and Its Revenue Implications" (unpublished; Washington: International Monetary Fund).

Alonso Gamo, Patricia, 1996, "The Association Agreement Between Lebanon and the EU: Issues Involved and Their Implications" (unpublished; Washington: International Monetary Fund).

Brown, Drusilla K., Alan V. Deardorff, Alan K. Fox, and Robert M. Stern, 1995, "Computational Analysis of Goods and Services Liberalization in the Uruguay Round," Discussion Paper No. 379 (Ann Arbor: University of Michigan, Research Forum on International Economics, School of Public Policy).

Diwan, Ishac, 1997, "How Can Lebanon Benefit from the Euro-Med Initiative?" (unpublished; Washington: World Bank).

Galal, Ahmed, and Bernard Hoekman, eds., 1997, "Regional Partners in Global Markets: Limits and Possibilities of the Euro-Med Agreements" (London: Center for Economic Policy Research).

Guide for Investors in Lebanon, 1997, prepared with the support of the European Commission for the Conference on Opportunities for Investment in the Mediterranean Region, London, March 6–7.

Helbling, Thomas, 1996, "An Initial Empirical Assessment of the Budgetary Aspects of Lebanon's Association Agreement with the EU" (unpublished; Washington: International Monetary Fund).

Hoekman, Bernard, 1995, "Trading Blocs and Trading Systems: The Service Dimension," *Journal of Economic Integration,* Vol. 10 (March), pp. 1–31.

———, 1996, "Effective Protection and Tariff Revenue in the Transition to Free Trade with the EU" (unpublished; Washington: World Bank).

———, and Carlos Primo Braga, 1997, "Protection of Trade in Services," World Bank Policy Research Working Papers, No. 1747 (Washington: World Bank).

Jones, Ronald W., and Frances Raune, 1990, "Appraising the Options for International Trade in Services," *Oxford Economic Papers,* Vol. 42 (October), pp. 672–87.

Lawrence, Robert, 1997, "Preferential Trading Agreements: The Traditional and the New" in Ahmed Galal and Bernard Hoekman, eds., 1997, "*Regional Partners in Global Markets: Limits and Possibilities of the Euro-Med Agreements*" (London: Center for Economic Policy Research).

Martin, Will, 1996, "Assessing the Implications for Lebanon of Free Trade with the EU" (unpublished; Washington: World Bank).

cision to open up its markets to international competition for both the service product and the service factor. Given Lebanon's technological advantage in producing *S,* free trade in products and services will lead to Lebanon's specialization in services. Point C^*, in Figure 7.2, determines the rate of return of the specific factor used in services and the price of the sector product, both of which are determined in world markets. Curve II passes below C^* and indicates that Lebanon has a comparative advantage in producing services compared with manufacturing (i.e., Lebanon can produce the service product cheaper than p_s^* if it had to pay the service factor r_s^*). Free trade at all levels would imply that the service sector will dominate: if it can sell at p_s^* and has to pay r_s^*, it can afford to pay higher wage than the manufacturing sector. The decline in manufacturing and the rise in local wage rates[13] will shift curve II upward until it eventually it passes through point C^*, which is the final equilibrium point with Lebanon specializing in services.

Therefore, in the context of this simplified model, one can show that opening up trade in services is welfare-improving for Lebanon. This result does not depend on Lebanon's relative endowment of the specific factor. The magnitude of the benefits from the right to establish or the right to do business, how-

---

[13]Eventually wages will be given by:

$$w = \frac{p_s^* - a_{Ks}r_s^*}{a_{Ns}}.$$

Mohieldin, Mahmoud, 1997, "The Egypt-EU Partnership Agreement and Liberalization of Services" in Ahmed Galal and Bernard Hoekman, eds., 1997, *Regional Partners in Global Markets: Limits and Possibilities of the Euro-Med Agreements* (London: Center for Economic Policy Research).

Moukarbel, Isbandar, 1996, "The Proposed Free-Trade Agreement Between Lebanon and the EU Countries: Evaluation and Recommendations," *Dossier de l'Association des Banques du Liban,* 6 (Beirut: Banque du Liban).

Nsouli, Saleh, Amer Bisat, and Oussama Kanaan, 1996, "The European Union's New Mediterranean Strategy," *Finance & Development,* Vol. 33 (September), pp. 14–17.

Primo Braga, Carlos, 1996, "The Impact of the Internationalization of Services on Developing Countries," *Finance & Development,* Vol. 33 (March), pp. 34–37.

Saidi, Nasser, 1996, "Lebanon and the EU at the Cross-Roads: an Interim Assessment of the Partnership Agreement" (unpublished; Beirut: Banque du Liban).

———, 1997, "The Reconstruction of Lebanon as a Regional Hub" (unpublished; Beirut: Banque du Liban).

Schiff, Maurice, 1996, "Small Is Beautiful: Preferential Trade Agreements and the Impact of Country Size, Market Share, Efficiency, and Trade Policy," Policy Research Working Papers, No. 1668 (Washington: World Bank).

World Bank, 1996, "The Partnership Agreement with the EU: Implications and Policy Options" (Washington: World Bank).

———, and UNCTAD, 1994, *Liberalizing International Transactions in Services: A Handbook* (New York: United Nations).

Statistical Appendix

Table A1. Selected Social, Economic, and Financial Indicators

I. Social and Demographic Indicators

Surface area (sq km)	10,400
Population density (people per sq km)	391.5
Roads, paved (in percent)	95

Population

Population, total	4,005,000
Labor force, total	1,314,688
Labor force growth, total (annual percent)	2.97
Population growth (annual percent)	1.90
Urban population (percent of total)	87.20
Urban population growth (annual percent)	2.70
Age-dependency ratio (dependents to working-age population)	0.70
Fertility rate, total (births per woman)	2.83

Health

Life expectancy at birth, female (years)	71.2
Life expectancy at birth, male (years)	67.5
Life expectancy at birth, total (years)	68.2
Mortality rate, infant (per 1,000 live births)	31.5
Mortality rate, under 5 (per 1,000 live births)	40.0
Immunization, DPT (percent of children under 12 months)	92.0
Immunization, measles (percent of children under 12 months)	88.0

Education

Illiteracy rate, adult male (percent of males 15+)	5.30
Illiteracy rate, adult total (percent of people 15+)	7.60
Gross primary enrollment (percent of school age population)	115

Infrastructure

Personal computers (per 1,000 people)	12.5
Mobile phones (per 1,000 people)	30.0
Telephone mainlines (per 1,000 people)	82.4
Television sets (per 1,000 people)	268.4

II. Economic and Financial Indicators

	1992	1993	1994	1995	1996	Est. 1997
	(Annual percent change)					
National income and prices						
Real GDP[1]	4.5	7.0	8.0	6.5	4.0	4.0
Consumer prices (period average)	99.8	24.7	8.0	10.6	8.9	7.7
External sector						
Exports (f.o.b.) U.S. dollar basis	9.7	13.8	−1.2	20.7	−4.0	−17.9
Imports (f.o.b.) U.S. dollar basis	12.2	29.6	12.9	21.3	4.0	−1.4
Nominal effective exchange rate (− depreciation)	−38.4	0.5	10.8	−0.9	6.6	12.9
Real effective exchange rate (− depreciation)	3.5	24.5	8.0	3.9	12.2	18.1
Central government						
Revenue	73.5	63.0	20.9	35.3	16.5	6.2
Expenditure[2]	85.5	38.3	75.3	17.9	21.9	25.0
	(Change in percent of broad money at the beginning of period, unless indicated otherwise)					
Money and credit						
Domestic credit	68.0	13.7	22.8	18.0	24.2	23.8
Net credit to public sector	16.5	4.0	10.6	5.1	12.9	13.5
Credit to private sector	51.5	9.7	12.2	12.9	11.3	10.3
Broad money (money and quasi-money)	114.3	32.1	25.3	16.4	27.8	19.3
Velocity (nominal GDP over broad money)	0.80	0.84	0.78	0.79	0.70	0.66
Interest rates						
(end of period; three-month treasury bills)	13.0	17.2	13.5	16.0	14.3	13.1
	(In percent of GDP)					
Consumption[3]	...	132.0	125.1	120.7	117.4	111.0
Investment[3]	...	29.1	32.4	33.0	30.1	29.8
Central government						
Revenue	12.0	14.1	14.6	16.8	17.3	16.4
Expenditure[2]	23.4	23.4	35.1	35.2	37.9	42.2
Of which: capital expenditure	1.5	3.4	9.3	9.4	8.5	8.6
Overall balance (including grants)	−11.4	−7.7	−17.2	−18.0	−20.2	−25.5
Overall balance (excluding grants)	−11.4	−9.2	−20.5	−18.4	−20.6	−25.8

Table A1 *(concluded)*

	1992	1993	1994	1995	1996	Est. 1997
	(In percent of GDP)					
Gross public debt	49.0	48.5	69.4	78.1	98.9	102.7
Domestic	44.0	44.2	61.1	66.5	84.4	86.5
External	5.3	4.3	8.3	11.5	14.5	16.2
Public sector deposits	10.9	10.6	17.2	15.0	19.0	6.1
Net public debt	38.1	37.9	52.2	63.1	79.9	96.6
Exports (f.o.b.)	10.8	9.1	7.4	7.3	6.0	4.3
Imports (f.o.b.)	68.3	65.1	60.8	60.5	53.8	46.4
External current balance	−49.8	−49.0	−45.0	−41.3	−34.7	−28.3
	(In millions of U.S. dollars)					
External sector						
Exports, (f.o.b.)	601	684	676	816	783	642
Imports, (f.o.b.)	−3,786	−4,908	−5,541	−6,722	−6,992	−6,897
Private transfers	416	565	685	836	1,226	1,411
Current account balance	−2,763	−3,688	−4,100	−4,587	−4,507	−4,199
Overall balance (+ surplus)	54	1,170	1,131	256	786	420
Central bank liquid reserves (end of period)	1,448	2,220	3,840	4,487	5,886	5,932
(In months of current year's imports)	4.6	5.4	8.3	8.0	10.1	10.3
External public debt outstanding (end of period)	257	327	772	1,305	1,907	2,434
External debt-service payments	...	58	143	184	138	571
Principal	...	41	134	109	20	435
Interest	...	17	9	81	118	136
Debt service (as percent of current receipts)	...	3.5	7.2	6.4	4.0	15.3
	(Lebanese pounds per U.S. dollar)					
Exchange rate (period average)	1,713	1,741	1,680	1,621	1,571	1,539
(end of period)	1,838	1,711	1,647	1,596	1,552	1,527
	(In billions of Lebanese pounds)					
GDP[1]	9,499	13,122	15,305	18,028	20,417	22,878

Sources: Ministry of Finance; Banque du Liban (BdL); Council for Development and Reconstruction (CDR); World Bank, *Social Indicators of Development; World Development Indicators,* CD-ROM World Bank, February 1997; and IMF staff estimates.

[1] Based on BdL and IMF staff estimates.

[2] Starting in 1993, includes externally financed capital (reconstruction) expenditures by the Council for Development and Reconstruction.

[3] IMF staff estimates based on data provided by the authorities.

Table A2. Selected Indicators of Sectoral Economic Activity

Indicator	1992	1993	1994	1995	1996	1997
Nominal GDP (in billions of Lebanese pounds)	9,499	13,122	15,305	18,028	20,417	22,878
Real GDP (percent change)	4.5	7.0	8.0	6.5	4.0	4.0
Consumer prices (annual percent change)						
Period average	99.8	24.7	8.0	10.6	8.9	7.7
End of period	118.4	3.9	11.6	11.9	6.7	6.7
Coincident indicator (1993 = 100)	...	100.0	115.5	131.6	138.7	144.2
Exports, f.o.b. (in billions of Lebanese pounds)	...	785.9	913.3	1,060.3	1,156.5	1,104.4
Imports, c.i.f. (in billions of Lebanese pounds)	...	3,857.1	4,746.9	8,862.8	11,903.1	11,495.0
Electricity production (in million kwh)	4,033	4,170	4,593	5,009	7,492	8,364
Construction permits (in thousand square meters)	10,745	15,053	20,301	29,008	13,498	11,386
Cement deliveries (in thousand metric tons)	2,127	3,045	3,396	3,968	3,812	3,654
Port of Beirut (number of ships)	3,054	3,323	3,376	3,429	3,279	3,116
Beirut Airport (thousands of passengers)	1,044	1,294	1,489	1,673	1,715	2,007

Source: Data provided by the Lebanese authorities.

Table A3. Aggregate Demand

	1992[1]	1993	1994	1995	1996
	(In billions of Lebanese pounds at current prices)				
Nominal GDP (market prices)	9,499	13,122	15,305	18,028	20,417
Resource gap[2]	−6,125	−8,021	−8,794	−9,664	−9,713
Gross domestic expenditure	15,624	21,142	24,099	27,691	30,130
Consumption	...	17,324	19,142	21,751	23,976
Private	...	15,820	17,261	19,521	21,419
Government	...	1,504	1,881	2,230	2,557
Gross domestic investment	...	3,818	4,957	5,941	6,155
Private	...	3,373	3,532	4,239	4,425
Public	...	445	1,425	1,702	1,730
Domestic savings	...	−4,203	−3,837	−3,723	−3,558
Public[3]	...	−739	−1,697	−1,476	−2,284
Private	...	−3,464	−2,140	−2,247	−1,274
	(In percent of GDP)				
Nominal GDP	100.0	100.0	100.0	100.0	100.0
Resource gap[2]	−64.5	−61.1	−57.5	−53.6	47.6
Gross domestic expenditure	164.5	161.1	157.5	153.6	147.6
Consumption	...	132.0	125.1	120.7	117.4
Private	...	120.6	112.8	108.3	104.9
Government	...	11.5	12.3	12.4	12.5
Gross domestic investment	...	29.1	32.4	33.0	30.1
Private	...	25.7	23.1	23.5	21.7
Public	...	3.4	9.3	9.4	8.5
Domestic savings	...	−32.0	−25.1	−20.7	−17.4
Public[3]	...	−5.6	−11.1	−8.2	−11.2
Private	...	−26.4	−14.0	−12.5	−6.2

Sources: Data provided by the Lebanese authorities; and IMF staff estimates.

[1] In view of the serious data problems for the year 1992, no staff estimates for the domestic expenditure items are provided.

[2] Net exports of goods and nonfactor services.

[3] Fiscal current account deficit excluding external interest payments.

Table A4. Consumer Price Index[1]
(Average for 1988 = 100)

	Index (Period average)	Annual Rate of Change[2] (In percent)
1991	435.6	50.1
1992	870.5	99.8
1993	1085.3	24.7
1994	1,171.8	8.0
1995	1,295.8	10.6
1996	1,411.3	8.9
1997	1,520.6	7.7
1996		
January	1,355.0	13.2
February	1,340.0	6.4
March	1,376.0	6.8
April	1,381.0	6.3
May	1,383.8	8.2
June	1,458.6	11.4
July	1,450.5	9.6
August	1,441.6	7.3
September	1,465.5	12.1
October	1,446.6	10.5
November	1,424.7	8.7
December	1,411.8	6.7
1997		
January	1,453.0	7.2
February	1,489.0	11.1
March	1,507.0	9.5
April	1,505.0	9.0
May	1,538.7	11.2
June	1,565.5	7.3
July	1,563.5	7.8
August	1,583.6	9.9
September	1,534.5	4.7
October	1,501.6	3.8
November	1,498.7	5.2
December	1,506.8	6.7

Source: Data provided by the Lebanese authorities.

[1]Based on an index for Beirut and suburbs prepared by the Consultation and Research Institute for the Trade Union Confederation.

[2]Annual data are averaged over the calendar year, while monthly data represent changes with respect to the same month in the previous year.

Table A5. Real Wages and Unit Labor Costs

	Real Minimum Wage (1990 = 100)	Real Average Wage[1] (1990 = 100)	GDP (In billions of Lebanese pounds, 1990 prices)	Labor Force (In million)	Average Labor Productivity (1990 = 100)	Real Unit Labor Costs[2] (1990 = 100)
1974	448	...	5,968	0.747	370	...
1975	460	...	5,005	0.771	301	...
1977	400	747	3,559	0.759	217	...
1980	386	678	3,603	0.742	225	...
1981	383	653	3,623	0.747	225	...
1982	374	644	2,290	0.753	141	...
1983	414	661	2,810	0.758	172	...
1984	404	618	4,060	0.764	246	...
1985	284	438	5,046	0.769	304	...
1986	261	376	4,704	0.796	274	...
1987	111	162	5,491	0.824	309	...
1988	113	162	3,942	0.853	214	...
1989	169	169	2,279	0.883	120	...
1990	100	100	1,973	0.914	100	100
1991	110	133	2,727	0.940	135	99
1992	79	97	2,849	0.966	137	71
1993	61	75	3,049	0.992	142	53
1994	96	113	3,293	1.022	149	76
1995	108	123	3,507	1.053	154	80
1996	119	122	3,647	1.074	157	77

Sources: Bank of Lebanon; *Investor's Guide: Lebanon 95* (Beirut: ECE, Études et Consultations Économiques, 1995); IBRD; and IMF staff estimates.
[1] The value for 1996 is estimated on the basis of the average monthly salary in the banking sector.
[2] Based on real average wage.

Table A6. Government Operations[1]

	1992	1993	1994	1995	Budget 1996	1996	Budget 1997	Est. 1997
	(In billions of Lebanese pounds)							
Revenue	1,138	1,855	2,242	3,033	4,022	3,534	4,100	3,753
Tax revenue	513	1,220	1,440	2,000	3,055	2,869	3,152	2,893
Indirect taxes	467	987	1,172	1,706	2,540	2,549	2,647	2,443
Of which: customs duties[2]	323	661	791	1,320	1,800	1,632	1,800	1,722
Of which: real estate transaction tax	...	177	197	222	275	260	275	291
Direct taxes	46	233	268	295	515	319	505	451
Of which: income tax	...	201	240	228	350	257	375	375
Nontax revenue[3]	626	635	802	1,033	967	665	948	860
Expenditure	2,219	3,069	5,379	6,342	7,248	7,732	6,963	9,662
Current expenditure	2,073	2,624	3,954	4,640	5,553	6,002	5,825	7,695
Wages and salaries	660	1,295	1,710	1,869	2,242	2,261	2,261	2,466
EDL fuel subsidy[4]	145	...	246	217	200	200	0	150
Other current[5]	750	545	510	678	511	888	864	1,701
Interest payments	519	784	1,488	1,875	2,600	2,653	2,700	3,378
Domestic	454	754	1,472	1,745	2,250	2,468	2,500	3,222
Foreign	65	30	15	131	350	185	200	155
Capital expenditure[6]	146	445	1,425	1,702	1,695	1,730	1,138	1,967
Of which: foreign financed	...	52	175	486	790	507	530	500
Overall balance (excluding grants)	−1,081	−1,214	−3,137	−3,309	−3,226	−4,198	−2,863	−5,909
Financing	979	1,288	3,130	3,345	3,226	5,003	2,863	6,142
Foreign	−108	346	1,192	892	1,087	943	1,232	792
Grants	0	197	507	73	300	71	...	72
Net borrowing[7]	−108	149	696	819	787	872	...	720
Disbursements	0	221	847	994	823	903	...	1,389
Amortization	−108	−72	−151	−176	−37	−31	...	−669
Domestic	1,087	942	1,938	2,453	2,139	4,060	1,631	5,350
Banking system	1,055	752	1,247	1,002	1,694	2,948	...	3,936
Banque du Liban	−668	−118	−1,545	−33	...	−1,145	...	2,693
Commercial banks	1,722	870	2,792	1,035	...	4,087	...	1,243
Nonbank private	32	190	691	1,452	445	1,118	...	1,414
Discrepancy[8]	−101	74	−8	36	0	805	0	233
	(In percent of GDP)							
Revenue	12.0	14.1	14.6	16.8	19.0	17.3	17.2	16.4
Tax revenue	5.4	9.3	9.4	11.1	14.5	14.0	13.2	12.6
Indirect taxes	4.9	7.5	7.7	9.5	12.0	12.5	11.1	10.7
Of which: customs duties[2]	3.4	5.0	5.2	7.3	8.5	8.0	7.6	7.5
Of which: real estate transaction tax	...	1.3	1.3	1.2	1.3	1.3	1.2	1.2
Direct taxes	0.5	1.8	1.8	1.6	2.4	1.6	2.1	2.0
Of which: income tax	...	1.5	1.6	1.3	1.7	1.3	1.6	1.6
Expenditure	23.4	23.4	35.1	35.2	34.3	37.9	29.2	42.2
Current expenditure (excluding interest payments)	16.4	14.0	16.1	15.3	14.0	16.4	13.1	18.9
Interest payments	5.5	6.0	9.7	10.4	12.3	13.0	11.3	14.8
Capital expenditure	1.5	3.4	9.3	9.4	8.0	8.5	4.8	8.6
Overall balance (excluding grants)	−9.2	−9.2	−20.5	−18.4	−15.3	−20.6	−12.0	−25.8
Overall balance (including grants)	−11.4	−7.7	−17.2	−18.0	−13.9	−20.2	...	−25.5
Current balance	−9.8	−5.9	−11.2	−8.9	−7.2	−12.1	−7.2	−17.2
Primary balance	−5.9	−3.3	−10.8	−8.0	−3.0	−7.6	−0.7	−11.1
Primary balance (excluding foreign financed investment)	...	−2.9	−9.6	−5.3	0.8	−5.1	1.5	−8.9
Domestic financing	11.4	7.2	12.7	13.9	10.1	20.0	6.8	23.4

Table A6 *(concluded)*

	1992	1993	1994	1995	Budget 1996	1996	Budget 1997	Est. 1997
					(In percent)			
Memorandum items								
Interest payments/total revenue	45.6	42.2	66.4	61.8	64.6	75.1	65.9	90.0
Custom duties/total revenue	28.4	35.7	35.3	43.5	44.8	46.2	43.9	45.9
Revenue/total expenditure	51.3	60.4	41.7	47.8	55.5	45.7	58.9	38.8
Overall balance/total expenditure	−48.7	−39.6	−58.3	−52.2	−44.5	−54.3	−41.1	−61.2
GDP (in billions of Lebanese pounds)	9,499	13,122	15,305	18,028	21,122	20,417	23,840	22,878

Sources: Ministry of Finance; Banque du Liban; Council for Development and Reconstruction (CDR); and IMF staff estimates.

[1]Includes the treasury and the foreign and domestically financed CDR capital expenditure. Other public entities are included on a net basis only.

[2]In July 1995, after the tariff reform, several excise taxes on imported goods started to be collected at the customs.

[3]Includes revenue from the lottery, collection from various tax penalties, and other fees and nontax revenue.

[4]Petroleum subsidy paid to the Electricity Company of Lebanon (EDL).

[5]Including advances and transfers.

[6]In 1996, this item includes domestically financed LL 151 billion of exceptional capital expenditure to rehabilitate the damages in 1996 caused by the bombings in April.

[7]Includes external loans to CDR and foreign currency bonds issued by the Lebanese Republic.

[8]Discrepancy between deficit and financing. The budget figures are recorded on a cash basis, while credit to the public sector is on the basis of the actual market value of the outstanding debt, that is, including accrued interest. In 1996, changes in accrued interest amounted to LL 506 billion, that is, about 70 percent of the discrepancy.

Table A7. Public Debt

	1992	1993	1994	1995	1996	1997
	(In billions of Lebanese pounds; end of period)					
Gross public debt	4,651	6,363	10,619	14,079	20,189	23,504
Gross domestic public debt	4,178	5,804	9,348	11,997	17,229	19,787
Of which: treasury bills and bonds[1]	4,018	5,739	9,266	11,838	17,022	19,578
Banque du Liban	284	454	105	195	124	375
Treasury bills and bonds[2]	139	392	27	92	24	274
Other	145	62	78	103	100	101
Commercial banks and financial institutions	3,099	4,245	7,345	8,453	12,638	15,532
Treasury bills and bonds[2]	3,083	4,242	7,341	8,397	12,532	13,424
Other	16	3	4	57	106	109
Nonbank private and other (treasury bills)	796	1,105	1,878	3,349	4,467	5,880
Gross external public debt[3]	473	560	1,271	2,082	2,960	3,717
Disbursements	0	221	847	994	903	1,389
Debt-service payments	...	102	166	307	218	824
Amortization	...	72	151	176	31	669
Interest payments	65	30	15	131	185	155
Public sector deposits	1,034	1,389	2,639	2,710	3,871	1,406
Net public debt[4]	3,618	4,974	7,983	11,369	16,318	22,098
	(In percent of GDP)					
Memorandum items						
Gross public debt	49.0	48.5	69.4	78.1	98.9	102.7
Domestic	44.0	44.2	61.1	66.5	84.4	86.5
External	5.0	4.3	8.3	11.5	14.1	16.2
Net public debt	38.1	37.9	52.2	63.1	79.9	96.6
GDP (in billions of Lebanese pounds)	9,499	13,122	15,305	18,028	20,417	22,878

Sources: Banque du Liban, various publications; IMF, *International Financial Statistics*; and IMF staff estimates.

[1] Face value of the outstanding treasury bills and bonds, and accrued interest on 24-month treasury bonds.

[2] Including treasury bill holdings resulting from repurchase agreements.

[3] The stock of external public debt is valued at the end-of-period exchange rate. Some discrepancies may arise because new disbursements and amortization payments are valued at the exchange rate of the time when the transaction took place.

[4] Defined as gross public debt minus public sector deposits with the banking system.

Table A8. Treasury Bills in Circulation[1]

(In millions of Lebanese pounds)

Type of Bills	1992	1993	1994	1995	1996	1997
Three-month						
Issue	2,031.2	2,525.4	1,393.0	3,776.3	4,716.8	2,360.6
Reimbursement	1,077.4	3,051.3	1,725.0	3,173.0	4,679.3	2,843.9
In circulation (end of period)	1,123.9	598.0	266.0	869.3	906.8	423.5
Six-month						
Issue	863.3	1,542.8	1,704.8	1,746.5	3,786.6	3,135.0
Reimbursement	469.9	1,294.9	1,764.7	1,751.7	2,116.6	4,755.0
In circulation (end of period)	629.3	877.2	817.3	812.1	2,482.1	861.6
Twelve-month						
Issue	1,184.6	1,769.3	2,940.8	6,607.0	5,001.2	5,833.0
Reimbursement	1,487.3	1,177.6	1,809.2	3,250.5	6,805.1	5,312.5
In circulation (end of period)	1,177.6	1,769.3	2,900.9	6,257.4	4,453.5	4,974.0
Eighteen-month						
Issue	164.8	—	—	—	—	—
Reimbursement	—	95.7	126.2	—	—	—
In circulation (end of period)	221.9	126.2	—	—	—	—
Twenty-four-month						
Issue	1,161.9	1,366.9	3,751.5	1,382.0	8,207.6	5,505.9
Reimbursement	—	350.6	1,254.3	1,758.2	4,016.7	1,909.9
In circulation (end of period)	1,506.3	2,522.5	5,019.8	4,643.5	8,834.5	12,430.5
Special bills[2]						
Issue	120.0	238.8	432.6	438.3	671.6	1,126.6
Reimbursement	70.1	203.1	326.3	443.0	527.5	813.2
In circulation (end of period)	95.4	131.1	237.3	232.6	376.7	690.1
Total bills						
Issue	5,525.9	7,443.3	10,222.7	13,950.1	22,383.8	17,961.1
Reimbursement	3,104.6	6,173.3	7,005.6	10,376.4	18,145.2	15,634.5
In circulation (end of period)	4,754.4	6,024.4	9,241.3	12,815.0	17,053.6	19,379.7

Source: Banque du Liban.

[1]Treasury bills in circulation at face value.

[2]Including special bills that can be part of the reserve requirement. Three percent of commercial banks' deposits have to be held as reserves in the form of such bills, which earn a fixed interest rate of 6 percent a year.

Table A9. Central Bank Balance Sheet
(End-of-period stocks; in billions of Lebanese pounds)

	1992	1993	1994	1995	1996	1997
Assets						
Foreign assets	8,369	10,051	12,236	12,953	14,516	13,222
Gold	5,636	6,166	5,821	5,701	5,292	4,078
Foreign exchange	2,661	3,816	6,342	7,179	9,152	9,075
Reserve and SDR positions	72	69	73	74	72	69
Claims on public sector	73	–7	5	29	29	325
Claims on private sector	37	44	73	106	96	122
Claims on commercial banks	164	154	85	233	105	97
Securities portfolio	0	491	118	97	331	466
Unclassified and fixed assets	296	227	337	449	478	513
Assets = liabilities	8,939	10,959	12,853	13,866	15,554	14,745
Liabilities						
Reserve money	1,514	2,154	3,811	4,618	5,580	8,370
Currency outside banks	798	715	939	1,046	1,161	1,210
Currency held by banks	44	49	67	82	96	115
Commercial bank deposits	672	1,390	2,805	3,490	4,323	7,045
Public sector deposits	928	1,237	2,384	2,441	3,586	1,189
Of which: foreign currency deposits	107	157	152	114	173	163
Liabilities to government from increase in pound value of foreign assets due to depreciation of the Lebanese pound	6,253	6,630	6,094	5,912	5,223	3,616
Foreign liabilities	6	10	50	115	85	112
Capital accounts	80	96	89	134	313	328
Unclassified liabilities	159	832	427	647	768	1,128

Source: Banque du Liban.

Table A10. Commercial Banks' Balance Sheet
(End of period stocks; in billions of Lebanese pounds)

	1992	1993	1994	1995	1996	1997
Assets						
Reserves	669	1,435	2,786	3,542	4,378	6,225
Currency	44	49	67	82	96	115
Deposits with Banque du Liban	625	1,386	2,719	3,460	4,282	6,110
Claims on private sector	4,804	5,898	7,800	10,320	12,687	15,451
Lebanese pounds	436	632	1,018	1,278	1,623	1,987
Foreign currency	4,368	5,266	6,782	9,042	11,064	13,464
Claims on public sector	3,098	4,013	6,909	7,949	12,060	13,234
Treasury bills	3,083	4,010	6,905	7,892	11,954	13,125
Other	16	3	4	57	106	109
Foreign assets	5,825	7,041	6,269	6,337	6,719	9,184
Fixed assets	144	259	406	739	1,151	1,272
Unclassified assets	94	164	115	169	188	267
Assets = liabilities	14,634	18,809	24,285	29,055	37,183	45,633
Liabilities						
Private sector deposits	11,062	14,409	18,686	21,806	27,505	33,307
Lebanese pounds	3,587	4,588	7,643	8,601	12,816	13,277
Sight	394	422	493	508	569	686
Term	3,194	4,165	7,150	8,093	12,247	12,592
Foreign currency	7,475	9,821	11,044	13,205	14,689	20,030
Sight	1,238	3,172	3,106	3,140	3,146	3,524
Term	6,237	6,650	7,938	10,065	11,543	16,506
Public sector deposits	107	152	255	261	285	217
Liabilities to nonresident banks	599	658	938	1,215	1,460	1,135
Deposits of nonresidents	1,100	1,393	1,663	2,078	3,180	5,262
In Lebanese pounds	134	157	201	393	535	658
Bonds	—	—	—	—	326	328
Capital accounts	264	444	676	1,146	1,944	2,990
Of which: subordinated loans[1]	48	30	25	21	33	147
Unclassified liabilities	1,504	1,753	2,066	2,549	2,484	2,394

Source: Banque du Liban.

[1]Subordinated loans to the banking system by nonresidents.

Table A11. Monetary Survey

	1992	1993	1994	1995	1996	1997
	(End-of-period stocks; in billions of Lebanese pounds)					
Total liquidity (M3)	11,870	15,678	19,651	22,883	29,241	34,898
Money (M1)	1,199	1,143	1,437	1,561	1,753	1,935
Currency	798	715	939	1,046	1,161	1,210
Demand deposits in domestic currency	401	429	498	514	593	725
Quasi-money	10,670	14,535	18,214	21,323	27,162	32,634
Domestic currency time and savings deposits	3,194	4,165	7,150	8,103	12,248	12,595
Foreign currency deposits	7,476	10,370	11,065	13,220	14,913	20,040
Bonds issued by banks	—	—	—	—	326	328
Net foreign assets[1]	12,441	15,000	15,829	15,862	16,477	15,750
Domestic credit	6,978	8,610	12,183	15,716	21,244	28,192
Net credit to public sector	2,138	2,617	4,275	5,276	8,218	12,154
Central bank	−854	−1,244	−2,378	−2,412	−3,557	−864
Commercial banks	2,992	3,862	6,653	7,688	11,775	13,01
Credit to private sector	4,841	5,992	7,908	10,440	13,026	16,039
Lebanese pounds	473	726	1,126	1,398	1,725	2,214
Foreign currency	4,368	5,266	6,782	9,042	11,300	13,824
Other items (net)	−7,550	−7,931	−8,361	−8,694	−8,480	−9,044
	(Change in percent of total liquidity at beginning of period)					
Total liquidity (M3)	114.3	32.1	25.3	16.4	27.8	19.3
Net foreign assets	113.7	21.6	5.3	0.2	2.7	−2.5
Net credit to public sector	16.5	4.0	10.6	5.1	12.9	13.5
Credit to private sector	51.5	9.7	12.2	12.9	11.3	10.3
Other items (net)	−67.4	−3.2	−2.7	−1.7	0.9	−1.9
	(In billions of Lebanese pounds; unless otherwise stated)					
Memorandum items						
Lebanese pound component of liquidity	4,393	5,309	8,587	9,663	14,002	14,530
Treasury bills held by nonbanks	814	1,110	1,898	3,349	4,467	5,878
M4 (M3 and treasury bills held by nonbanks)	12,684	16,788	21,549	26,233	33,708	40,776
Credit to public sector (12-month change)	74.9	22.4	63.3	23.4	55.8	47.9
Credit to private sector (12-month change)	143.2	23.8	32.0	32.0	24.8	23.1
Foreign currency deposits as share of M3	63.0	66.1	56.3	57.8	51.0	57.4
Foreign currency lending/total private lending	90.2	87.9	85.8	86.6	86.8	86.2
Interest rate (3-month treasury bill yield), end of period	13.0	17.2	13.5	16.0	14.3	13.1
Real interest rate[2]	−105.4	13.3	1.9	4.1	7.6	6.4
Income velocity of total liquidity	0.80	0.84	0.78	0.79	0.70	0.66
Credit to private sector (in percent of GDP)	51.0	45.3	51.4	57.8	63.8	70.1

Source: Banque du Liban.

[1]Including IMF reserve position.

[2]Treasury bill yield (3 months) minus inflation rate (over preceding 12 months), all at end of period.

Table A12. Factors Affecting Changes in Total Liquidity (M3)

	1992	1993	1994	1995	1996	1997
	(In billions of Lebanese pounds)					
Total liquidity (M3)	6,331	3,809	3,973	3,232	6,358	5,657
Net foreign assets	6,299	2,586	802	33	616	−727
Domestic credit	3,766	1,631	3,573	3,533	5,528	6,948
Net credit to public sector	915	480	1,658	1,001	2,942	3,936
Central bank	−933	−390	−1,134	−33	−1,145	2,693
Commercial banks	1,722	870	2,792	1,035	4,087	1,243
Credit to private sector	2,851	1,152	1,915	2,532	2,586	3,013
Lebanese pounds	111	253	400	272	327	489
Foreign currency	2,740	899	1,515	2,260	2,259	2,524
Other items (net)	−3,735	−381	−430	−334	214	−564
	(Changes in percent of beginning of period stock of liquidity)					
Total liquidity (M3)	114.3	32.1	25.3	16.4	27.8	19.3
Net foreign assets	113.7	21.6	5.3	0.2	2.7	−2.5
Domestic credit	68.0	13.7	22.8	18.0	24.2	23.8
Net credit to public sector	16.5	4.0	10.6	5.1	12.9	13.5
Central bank	−16.8	−3.3	−7.2	−0.2	−5.0	9.2
Commercial banks	31.1	7.3	17.8	5.3	17.9	4.3
Credit to private sector	51.5	9.7	12.2	12.9	11.3	10.3
Lebanese pounds	2.0	2.1	2.6	1.4	1.4	1.7
Foreign currency	49.5	7.6	9.7	11.5	9.9	8.6
Other items (net)	−67.4	−3.2	−2.7	−1.7	0.9	−1.9

Sources: Banque du Liban; and IMF staff calculations.

Table A13. Discounts and Yields on Three-Month Treasury Bills
(End of period; in percent a year)

	Primary Market		Secondary Market	
	Discount	Yield	Discount	Yield
1992				
March	22.50	23.84	22.50	23.84
June	22.50	23.84	22.50	23.84
September	31.50	34.18	33.50	36.55
December	12.59	13.00	12.59	13.00
1993				
March	19.96	21.01	19.96	21.01
June	17.67	18.48	17.67	18.48
September	17.28	18.06	17.28	18.06
December	16.51	17.22	16.51	17.22
1994				
March	15.69	16.33	15.69	16.33
June	14.74	15.30	14.74	15.30
September	13.97	14.47	13.97	14.47
December	13.05	13.49	13.05	13.49
1995				
March	15.89	16.55	15.89	16.55
June	19.00	19.94	19.00	19.94
September	23.80	25.30	23.50	25.30
December	15.40	16.01	15.40	16.01
1996				
March	15.21	15.81	15.21	15.81
June	14.98	15.56	14.98	15.56
September	14.10	14.61	14.10	14.61
December	13.80	14.29	13.80	14.29
1997				
March	13.29	13.75	13.29	13.75
June	12.97	13.40	12.97	13.40
September	12.68	13.09	...	...
December	12.68	13.09	...	...

Source: Banque du Liban.

Table A14. Commercial Bank Interest Rates on Lebanese Pound Transactions[1]
(In percent)

	Lending Rates[2] Discount and loans	Deposit Rates[2]				Interbank Rates on Call		
		Checking and current accounts	Savings at call	Term Savings and deposits	Average rate	Lowest rate during the period	Highest rate during the period	End-of-period rate
1991	31.54	3.74	11.83	15.37	13.81	9.50	12.00	12.00
1992	27.45	1.50	8.34	14.26	11.48	3.00	5.00	5.00
1993	29.29	1.88	10.43	16.10	13.18	6.00	6.00	6.00
1994	21.28	2.23	8.13	13.87	12.79	6.00	53.00	13.50
1995	28.99	4.28	11.56	18.23	17.12	9.00	15.00	13.00
1996	24.68	4.24	10.06	15.36	14.69	10.00	25.00	15.50
1994								
March	27.35	2.02	10.35	15.75	13.60	6.00	10.00	8.00
June	23.09	2.61	9.37	14.70	12.72	6.00	8.00	6.00
September	22.01	2.45	8.80	14.19	13.13	6.00	10.00	6.00
December	21.28	2.23	8.13	13.87	12.79	6.00	53.00	13.50
1995								
March	21.32	3.69	11.13	14.51	13.75	9.00	14.00	9.50
June	22.76	4.43	10.75	15.24	14.26	6.00	40.00	7.00
September	27.63	3.56	12.29	17.27	15.68	15.00	100.00	15.00
December	28.99	4.28	11.56	18.23	17.12	9.00	15.00	13.00
1996								
March	25.95	3.96	10.84	15.52	14.69	10.00	13.00	10.00
June	24.99	3.96	11.09	15.17	14.41	10.00	12.00	10.50
September	24.43	4.37	10.05	15.35	14.40	9.00	11.00	10.00
December	24.68	4.24	10.06	15.36	14.69	10.00	25.00	15.50
1997								
March	20.47	3.17	9.96	13.56	12.87	9.00	11.00	10.00
June	19.86	2.94	9.17	13.08	12.41	9.00	10.50	9.50
September	19.36	2.33	9.20	12.87	12.16	9.00	50.00	45.00
December	20.28	2.67	9.02	13.72	12.97	9.00	13.00	12.75

Sources: Banque du Liban; and Société Financière du Liban.
[1]End-of-period interest rates.
[2]Weighted average.

Table A15. Balance of Payments

	1992	1993	1994	1995	1996	Est. 1997

(In millions of U.S. dollars)

	1992	1993	1994	1995	1996	Est. 1997
Current account	−2,763	−3,688	−4,100	−4,587	−4,507	...
Trade balance	−3,185	−4,224	−4,866	−5,906	−6,209	−6,255
Export f.o.b.[1]	601	684	676	816	783	642
Imports f.o.b.[1]	−3,786	−4,908	−5,541	−6,722	−6,992	−6,897
Services	−71	−142	31	438	425	...
Factor	320	240	400	492	399	...
Interest	14	37	125	128	148	...
Banque du Liban (net)	14	54	134	209	266	...
Interest on external public debt	...	−17	−9	−81	−118	...
Investment income	306	203	275	364	251	...
Commercial banks (net)	138	88	109	136	72	...
Earnings	214	155	165	250	220	...
Payments	−76	−67	−56	−114	−148	...
Nonbanks[2]	168	115	166	228	179	...
Earnings	231	169	260	336	322	...
Payments	−63	−54	−94	−108	−143	...
Nonfactor	−391	−382	−369	−54	26	...
Insurance and freight	−421	−427	−449	−545	−574	−559
Travel and transportation	30	45	80	91	150	...
Other services[3]	...	...	...	400	450	...
Unrequited transfers	493	678	735	881	1,277	...
Public	77	113	50	45	51	...
Private[4]	416	565	685	836	1,226	...
Capital account	2,817	4,858	5,231	4,843	5,293	...
Direct investment	...	1,811	2,100	2,933	2,552	...
External public disbursements	...	126	542	613	575	1,002
Contracted loans	...	127	142	313	475	366
Eurobond	...	0	400	300	100	636
Amortization on external public debt	−59	−41	−134	−103	−20	−435
Nonbank short-term capital[2]	610	790	110	450	186	...
Claims on foreign banks (−increase)	660	740	60	150	135	...
Liabilities to foreign banks	−50	50	50	300	51	...
Other capital[5]	2,266	2,173	2,613	950	2,060	...
Overall balance	54	1,170	1,131	256	786	420
Net foreign reserves (−increase)	−54	−1,170	−1,131	−256	−786	−420
Banque du Liban	−231	−456	−1,861	−591	−1,428	−62
Commercial banks	177	−714	730	335	642	−358

(In percent; unless indicated otherwise)

Memorandum items						
Current account balance/GDP	−49.8	−49.0	−45.0	−41.3	−34.7	−28.3
External public debt (in millions of U.S. dollars)	257	327	772	1,305	1,907	2,434
External public debt	4.6	4.3	8.3	11.5	14.5	16.2
Debt service (in millions of U.S. dollars)	...	58.4	143.3	189.3	137.5	571.0
Principal (in millions of U.S. dollars)	...	41.3	134.2	108.5	19.7	434.6
Interest (in millions of U.S. dollars)	...	17.1	9.1	80.8	117.8	136.4
Debt service/current receipts	...	3.5	7.2	6.4	4.0	15.3
Foreign exchange reserves (in millions of U.S. dollars)	1,448	2,220	3,840	4,487	5,886	5,932
Foreign exchange reserves (in months of imports)	4.6	5.4	8.3	8.0	10.1	10.3
GDP (in millions of U.S. dollars)	5,545	7,535	9,110	11,119	12,997	14,861

Sources: Banque du Liban; Council for Development and Reconstruction; Ministry of Finance; IMF, *Direction of Trade Statistics; International Financial Statistics;* and IMF staff estimates.

[1]For 1993, IMF, *Direction of Trade Statistics,* customs data thereafter. Export data were adjusted to reflect changes in valuation of transfers of banknotes abroad, previously included at face value.

[2]Data on the flow of international bank lending to nonbank residents of Lebanon and on the flow of deposits by residents of Lebanon with international banks are obtained from stock data provided by the Bank for International Settlement. For 1996, based on Q1 data. Estimates of interest payments and receipts are derived by applying the average three-month Eurodollar rate to the average stock.

[3]Includes information, construction, financial, business, medical, and communication services. Data available as of 1995.

[4]Includes government transfers. Data available as of 1996.

[5]Includes valuation adjustments and errors and omissions (mainly unrecorded flows of both current and capital account items).

Table A16. Composition of Industrial Exports[1]
(In percent of total)

	1992	1993	1994	1995	1996
Food and beverages	6.0	21.8	21.3	21.9	21.8
Textiles	14.0	16.7	13.3	12.4	12.5
Leather, plastics, and rubber	3.0	7.3	7.3	6.3	7.5
Wood and wood products	1.0	0.5	0.7	0.3	0.3
Chemicals and pharmaceuticals	35.0	7.3	8.3	7.3	4.7
Paper and paper products	6.0	4.3	5.0	6.9	6.5
Stone, clay, and glass	6.0	5.3	5.9	4.9	3.1
Metal and metal products	11.0	8.7	10.5	10.2	9.1
Machinery and appliances	8.0	15.2	13.8	15.6	20.4
Jewelry	3.0	8.9	10.2	10.6	11.1
Other	7.0	4.0	3.6	3.7	3.1
Total	100.0	100.0	100.0	100.0	100.0

Sources: For 1992, Beirut Chamber of Commerce and Industry; for 1993–96, Lebanon Directorate of Customs.

[1]Exports data were adjusted to reflect changes in the valuation of transfers of banknotes abroad, previously included at face value.

Table A17. Destination of Exports
(In percent of total)

	1992	1993	1994	1995	1996
Industrial countries	32.8	28.0	33.5	27.5	34.2
Italy	3.0	1.3	2.6	2.1	6.3
United States	4.6	3.7	3.5	2.6	4.2
Switzerland	8.0	7.8	13.3	2.9	1.9
France	5.3	4.0	4.5	6.9	7.1
Germany	2.4	1.4	2.0	2.6	3.0
United Kingdom	2.9	2.3	1.5	2.1	2.4
Other	6.5	7.6	6.1	8.2	9.3
Developing countries	67.2	72.0	66.5	72.5	65.8
Middle East	56.1	47.7	42.2	40.4	47.6
Saudi Arabia	17.8	14.5	13.9	11.2	18.1
Syrian Arab Republic	7.5	8.7	7.4	4.7	9.1
Jordan	7.2	4.6	3.5	2.1	6.6
United Arab Emirates	12.0	10.8	4.4	4.9	7.5
Other	19.1	17.8	20.3	22.2	15.3
Africa	5.1	3.2	3.3	3.6	4.9
Europe	0.7	2.5	1.3	2.7	3.5
Other	5.2	18.6	19.7	25.8	9.7
Total	100.0	100.0	100.0	100.0	100.0

Source: IMF, *Direction of Trade Statistics*. The direction of trade statistics data for Lebanon are based on trading partner records.

Table A18. Sources of Imports
(In percent of total)

	1992	1993	1994	1995	1996
Industrial countries	60.5	63.9	65.6	65.8	69.1
Italy	13.6	12.7	13.3	13.0	12.1
France	8.1	8.6	8.9	7.6	7.8
Germany	6.8	9.2	10.0	8.4	8.5
United States	8.1	10.6	9.3	10.6	10.9
Japan	3.6	3.8	4.2	3.9	3.9
United Kingdom	4.2	4.4	4.1	3.9	4.0
Switzerland	2.6	3.3	3.5	4.6	3.4
Belgium-Luxembourg	3.1	1.9	1.8	1.9	1.5
Other	10.5	9.3	10.4	12.0	17.0
Developing countries	39.5	36.1	34.4	34.2	30.9
Middle East	14.3	9.6	7.8	7.5	8.3
Saudi Arabia	0.7	1.4	1.4	0.7	1.5
Syrian Arab Republic	11.4	5.0	4.4	3.2	4.1
Other	2.2	3.2	2.0	3.5	2.7
Africa	0.5	2.8	2.5	2.2	1.0
Other	24.7	23.7	24.2	24.5	21.6
Total	100.0	100.0	100.0	100.0	100.0
Memorandum item					
European Union	44.7	48.2	50.8	51.6	...

Source: IMF, *Direction of Trade Statistics*. The direction of trade statistics data for Lebanon are based on trading partner records and include estimates, particularly for import, from developing countries.

Table A19. Exchange Rate of the Lebanese Pound

End of Period	Exchange Rate (In Lebanese Pounds per U.S. dollar)	Percent Change in U.S. Dollar/ Lebanese Pounds Rate Over Previous Year	Exchange Rate (In Lebanese Pounds per SDR)	Percent Change in SDR/ Lebanese Pounds Rate Over Previous Year
1992				
March	1,280.0	−26.7	1,755.8	−28.1
June	1,705.0	−47.0	2,440.1	−51.3
September	2,420.0	−63.2	3,564.3	−65.8
December	1,838.0	−52.2	2,527.3	−50.2
1993				
March	1,742.0	−26.5	2,434.8	−27.9
June	1,731.0	−1.5	2,429.6	0.4
September	1,723.5	40.4	2,444.6	45.8
December	1,711.0	7.4	2,350.2	7.5
1994				
March	1,694.5	2.8	2,393.7	1.7
June	1,680.0	3.0	2,433.3	−0.1
September	1,666.0	3.5	2,444.7	—
December	1,647.0	3.9	2,404.4	−2.3
1995				
March	1,634.5	3.7	2,550.6	−6.1
June	1,620.5	3.7	2,542.2	−4.3
September	1,610.5	3.4	2,425.9	−0.8
December	1,596.0	3.2	2,372.4	1.3
1996				
March	1,583.5	3.2	2,313.8	10.2
June	1,571.0	3.2	2,267.5	12.1
September	1,558.5	3.3	2,243.3	8.1
December	1,552.0	2.8	2,231.7	6.3
1997				
March	1,545.8	2.4	2,143.8	7.9
June	1,539.8	2.0	2,137.4	6.1
September	1,533.3	1.6	2,093.2	7.2
December	1,527.0	1.6	2,060.3	8.3

Source: IMF, *International Financial Statistics.*

Table A20. Nominal and Real Effective Exchange Rates of the Lebanese Pound
(1992 = 100, period averages)

	Nominal Effective Exchange Rate	Real Effective Exchange Rate
1992		
March	155.6	114.6
June	97.2	93.6
September	66.5	84.5
December	80.7	107.4
1993		
March	95.6	122.0
June	98.1	123.1
September	103.4	127.0
December	107.2	128.4
1994		
March	111.2	135.5
June	112.7	137.0
September	110.4	132.2
December	111.0	132.0
1995		
March	110.9	137.0
June	108.0	137.1
September	110.5	142.1
December	111.9	141.6
1996		
March	114.8	148.6
June	117.8	156.8
September	117.9	160.8
December	120.2	159.8
1997		
March	127.9	175.6
June	131.0	185.2
September	136.0	193.3
December	136.4	185.3

Source: IMF staff estimates.

Recent Occasional Papers of the International Monetary Fund

155. Fiscal Policy Issues During the Transition in Russia, by Augusto Lopez-Claros and Sergei V. Alexashenko. 1998.

154. Credibility Without Rules? Monetary Frameworks in the Post–Bretton Woods Era, by Carlo Cottarelli and Curzio Giannini. 1997.

153. Pension Regimes and Saving, by G.A. Mackenzie, Philip Gerson, and Alfredo Cuevas. 1997.

152. Hong Kong, China: Growth, Structural Change, and Economic Stability During the Transition, by John Dodsworth and Dubravko Mihaljek. 1997.

151. Currency Board Arrangements: Issues and Experiences, by a staff team led by Tomás J.T. Baliño and Charles Enoch. 1997.

150. Kuwait: From Reconstruction to Accumulation for Future Generations, by Nigel Andrew Chalk, Mohamed A. El-Erian, Susan J. Fennell, Alexei P. Kireyev, and John F. Wilson. 1997.

149. The Composition of Fiscal Adjustment and Growth: Lessons from Fiscal Reforms in Eight Economies, by G.A. Mackenzie, David W.H. Orsmond, and Philip R. Gerson. 1997.

148. Nigeria: Experience with Structural Adjustment, by Gary Moser, Scott Rogers, and Reinold van Til, with Robin Kibuka and Inutu Lukonga. 1997.

147. Aging Populations and Public Pension Schemes, by Sheetal K. Chand and Albert Jaeger. 1996.

146. Thailand: The Road to Sustained Growth, by Kalpana Kochhar, Louis Dicks-Mireaux, Balazs Horvath, Mauro Mecagni, Erik Offerdal, and Jianping Zhou. 1996.

145. Exchange Rate Movements and Their Impact on Trade and Investment in the APEC Region, by Takatoshi Ito, Peter Isard, Steven Symansky, and Tamim Bayoumi. 1996.

144. National Bank of Poland: The Road to Indirect Instruments, by Piero Ugolini. 1996.

143. Adjustment for Growth: The African Experience, by Michael T. Hadjimichael, Michael Nowak, Robert Sharer, and Amor Tahari. 1996.

142. Quasi-Fiscal Operations of Public Financial Institutions, by G.A. Mackenzie and Peter Stella. 1996.

141. Monetary and Exchange System Reforms in China: An Experiment in Gradualism, by Hassanali Mehran, Marc Quintyn, Tom Nordman, and Bernard Laurens. 1996.

140. Government Reform in New Zealand, by Graham C. Scott. 1996.

139. Reinvigorating Growth in Developing Countries: Lessons from Adjustment Policies in Eight Economies, by David Goldsbrough, Sharmini Coorey, Louis Dicks-Mireaux, Balazs Horvath, Kalpana Kochhar, Mauro Mecagni, Erik Offerdal, and Jianping Zhou. 1996.

138. Aftermath of the CFA Franc Devaluation, by Jean A.P. Clément, with Johannes Mueller, Stéphane Cossé, and Jean Le Dem. 1996.

137. The Lao People's Democratic Republic: Systemic Transformation and Adjustment, edited by Ichiro Otani and Chi Do Pham. 1996.

136. Jordan: Strategy for Adjustment and Growth, edited by Edouard Maciejewski and Ahsan Mansur. 1996.

135. Vietnam: Transition to a Market Economy, by John R. Dodsworth, Erich Spitäller, Michael Braulke, Keon Hyok Lee, Kenneth Miranda, Christian Mulder, Hisanobu Shishido, and Krishna Srinivasan. 1996.

134. India: Economic Reform and Growth, by Ajai Chopra, Charles Collyns, Richard Hemming, and Karen Parker with Woosik Chu and Oliver Fratzscher. 1995.

133. Policy Experiences and Issues in the Baltics, Russia, and Other Countries of the Former Soviet Union, edited by Daniel A. Citrin and Ashok K. Lahiri. 1995.

132. Financial Fragilities in Latin America: The 1980s and 1990s, by Liliana Rojas-Suárez and Steven R. Weisbrod. 1995.

131. Capital Account Convertibility: Review of Experience and Implications for IMF Policies, by staff teams headed by Peter J. Quirk and Owen Evans. 1995.

Note: For information on the title and availability of Occasional Papers not listed, please consult the IMF Publications Catalog or contact IMF Publication Services.